Untold Stories of the Exodus

Untold Stories of the Exodus

Pran Pandit

ZORBA BOOKS

ZORBA BOOKS

Published by Zorba Books, June 2022
Website: www.zorbabooks.com
Email: info@zorbabooks.com

Title :- Untold Stories of the Exodus

Printbook ISBN :- 978-93-93029-31-7
Ebook ISBN :- 978-93-93029-38-6

Zorba Books Pvt. Ltd. (opc)
Sushant Arcade,
Next to Courtyard Marriot,
Sushant Lok 1, Gurgaon – 122009, India

This book is dedicated to those bravehearts of the Jammu and Kashmir Police who sacrificed their lives for maintaining peace, order and security, and safeguarding the sovereignty and territorial integrity of India.

Contents

Foreword

I was delighted to go through the unpublished material of what eventually is going to hit bookstalls in the form of a book entitled 'Untold Stories of the Exodus'. I am not aware of any book on Kashmir, covering the same ground, in which the author has blended the material and memory so well.

Kashmir, the holy abode of *Shiva* and *Parvati*, the great seat of learning *Shaiv-Darshana* and *Tantra Shastra;* the land from where *Buddhism* spread to Ladakh, Tibet, China and the whole world; the valley of saints and sages, the birth place of spiritual and literary figures like 'Lal-Ded' and 'Sheikh Noor-ud-Din', who eluded the proprietorial claims of religious monopolists and nurtured humanity; and the cradle of *adyatmikta* and *Tasawuf,* where all religious faiths including *Islam* grew and proliferated for centuries, is at cross-roads today. After having become the reservoir of violence that stemmed from politics and religion-based terror, the devastating potentialities, aided, abetted and facilitated by the Islamic Republic of Pakistan, has undone all socio-economic and religio-cultural fine-ness of the region for which Kashmir and Kashmiris were known all over the world.

Kashmiri Pandits, the aborigines of the land, who first bore the brunt of terror networks that operated in the valley in the name of freeing the region from Indian sovereignty, were forced to abandon their homes and hearths. Enduring all humiliations and sufferings, taking along with them only the nostalgia of their homeland, they got sparsely spread beyond the geographical region of Kashmir.

I am pained to see that despite lapse of more than 32 years, the hounded out Kashmiri Pandit community members continue to live away from their roots, and except for inadequate doles, lip-service and occasional references, nothing tangible has been done by the successive state governments and the GOI in the direction of their honorable return and rehabilitation. It is quite heartening to see that the resilience shown by the most persecuted and globally scattered community, and their inherent ability to 'live and let live' and to 'bend and blend' has helped them to struggle through the vicissitudes for survival.

I am a student of History; and I find that the book entitled 'Untold Stories of the Exodus' has great merit. It is a pioneering exercise in thoroughly mapping the crisis scenario. The vivid description is successful on its own terms, and the author has succeeded in meeting the objectives of useful surveys of scholarship in Sociological study.

Pran Pandit, a former decorated Police officer, and thoroughly integrated with the civil society of Kashmir, has shown a rare flash of brilliance in bringing to fore the fact that Kashmiri Pandits' intellect is alive and well-groomed even after having been tossed to the ground so brutally. His gleanings are organized in ten real stories that stem from Pakistan's meddling in the affairs of Kashmiris in the name of religion.

Pandit has done a commendable job in sharing reliable and authentic record of one of the most critical and significant periods that future researchers on Kashmir would cherish and consult. He gives a fresh outlook on problems confronted by the hounded out community; and with meticulous clarity, excellent analysis and argumentation, he has packed a lot of valuable information in unpretentious prose. The complexity of the crisis faced by Kashmiri Pandits, presenting a synergistic and cross paradigm approach, is so well captured in the framework of the stories in the book. The book is a real eye opener for the intelligentsia and the policy makers.

The author has achieved what he has set out to accomplish with a rare frame of expression as well as conceptual clarity; and the empirical richness of the book shall be an important resource, not only for the students of social sciences, but also for the common man interested in understanding the fundamentals of structural changes occurring in different regions of the world for politico-diplomatic maneuvering through radicalization.

The tone of the book can be grasped by the introduction, demonstrating the quality of conceptually articulated varied perspectives, both local and global. The author's work is subtle in bringing to fore a convincing relief for academics and public in general of region's defaced culture; and the excellent introduction to the book is a model of its kind. The stories in the book qualify that Pakistan's thugs and their agents in the valley, who operate in religious clothing, in a variety of camouflaged ways, hounded out Kashmiri Pandits from their homeland.

The book is rich in style, deep in detail, and exhaustive in scope–a sound monograph and a painstaking investigation. Each story is built on layer upon layer of micro and macro perspectives. The observation is full of brewing ideas that can take thirst for new ideas in studying Kashmiri Pandit community's problems; and the most striking feature of this work is the persistent pattern of issues.

Although Pran Pandit has remained an officer connected with the security of the state and maintenance of law and order in Kashmir region, yet, I think, his narrative is not opinionated or based on 'Police files'. He has passionately recollected the situations, events and occurrences; and the characters like Hameed Bhai, Shakeel, Shamsher Khan, Gwash lal, Abimanyu, Rashid Khan, the distraught mother, Mohini, and Rohit, Mohit, Radha and others are over arching ends of the semantic spectrum.

It is a thoughtful book, a useful toolbox for empirical research and shall serve as catalyst for scholars to engage in a truly stimulating dialogue. I congratulate Pran Pandit for bringing out such a fine book.

– Professor Dr. Rattan Lal Hangloo
(Former Professor of History, Central University of Hyderabad, India; Former Vice Chancellor Kalyani University, West Bengal, India; Former Vice Chancellor University of Allahabad, Prayagraj, India; and Honorary Chancellor, Nobel International University, Toronto, Canada)

Introduction

From time immemorial, Kashmir has been the beloved homeland of my forbears. I was born, brought up and nourished in Kashmir; my religious faith, mother tongue, cultural traditions, practices and beliefs are deeply rooted in Kashmir; and my unique ethnic identity is '*Kashmiri Batta',* Kashmiri Pundit!

Kashmir, as I have seen in the hay days, was an example of social cohesion. It shall not be over emphasizing the fact that despite differing religious beliefs, Hindus and Muslims, the two main religious communities of Kashmir, lived in perfect amity, in an atmosphere of trust and confidence; and the natives of the land shared cultural traditions, including religious and social rites and rituals. My treasured memories of the bygone days make me ecstatically happy, but my heart bleeds to see the changed social structure of my homeland due to the en masse exodus of minuscule minority community members, the aborigines of the land!

I think that most of the people world over don't know that more than three decades ago, Kashmir was engulfed in flames of terror, and the civil society of the beautiful vale was thrown into a bizarre situation of 'every man for himself' by the perpetrators of mayhem. They are unaware of the fact that the natives of Kashmir, savaged by the beasts in the shape of men, continue to live in fear to this day.

The present-day inhabitants of Kashmir valley, mostly the descendents of the aborigines of land, have a notable genetic character trait of watching and observing the neighborhood meticulously in the manner dolphins do, with one eye open even in sleep; and with great attention, they have watched the signs and symptoms of a dangerous situation in-making including the fanning of the brutal and violent flames of 'terror' in their homeland.

I am solidly grounded in the belief that the people born and living in a particular area or region are in a much better position than others to explicate a clearer picture of demographics, social milieu, changing tides and emerging issues in their native land because of their familiarity with the people and knowledge regarding the race, ethnicity, religious, cultural and other information of the area. They can give an authentic account of the events, happenings and developments, which may have unfolded under their nose.

I chose to bring out a book on an intricate subject related to Kashmir imbroglio, and that is not for no reason. Immersing myself in reading Kashmir history, authored by various authors, mythological texts and didactic material, to uncover various facets of life of the people of Kashmir, and minutely observing the surroundings has been my disposition all my life; and I wanted to give things away to others in a 'Snow White' manner, bereft of bias and concoction. I am grounded in firm belief that any growing scenario is better understood by observing the situation directly and obliquely with painstaking attention by using the power of perspective. I hold to the view that 'truth' is intimately related to observation and experience; and the hard-nosed recounting of the facts is 'unvarnished truth'.

I had been regularly interacting with the people, observing and analyzing the events and developments around to the hilt, and that helped me comprehend the social dynamics and emerging situations of my homeland. Many memories of my homeland are as vivid to me today as they were about fifty years back; and I do reminisce with clarity, like the glacier-water running down a mountain, the dark clouds of hatred and intolerance fluttering under the gaze of the fascinating blue skies of the valley, including the activities of religious fundamentalists and separatists, which sent strong signals, louder than words, of impending trouble in Kashmir.

Towards the beginning of 1980, with a view to replacing the 'ethos of pluralistic culture' and 'humanistic traditions of Sufis and Saints by a rigid and distorted version of religious faith, members of *Jammat-e-Islamia*, a pro-Pakistan extremist organization in Kashmir, had busied themselves in creating rancor against the traditional way of life and inspirational secular values of the natives of the land by spreading canard against the centuries-old unique culture and ethos of Kashmir. They were hell-bent on dismantling the solid foundations of '*Kashmiriyat*' because they perceived it as a major stumbling block in radicalizing and hardening the beliefs of Kashmiri Muslims. The sympathizers of *Jammat-e-Islamia* had embarked on the journey of propagating a fallacious opinion that the unique and traditional way of life of the Muslims of Kashmir, seeped with mysticism and devotional Sufi-order, was not conforming to 'Islamic tenets'; and Kashmir's changing face, from 'moderate' to 'radical', appeared imminent.

A section of the population of Kashmir, comprising the radicalized youth, numerically small though, religious zealots, psychologically maladjusted and intellectually dwarf, after pledging their support to separatist elements, patronized and aided by the Islamic Republic of Pakistan, had engaged themselves in promoting narrow grooves of prejudice and contradictions in basic tenets of religion and humanity for eroding the indigenous character of Kashmir. Antinational elements and windbags were busy portraying the image of Pakistan as a messiah of Muslims world over including the Muslims of the state of Jammu and Kashmir, besides spreading blind prejudices and vituperation to create hatred and dissatisfaction against India; and their machinations were easy discernible.

Around 1985, 'seeds of radicalization' were sprouting on the ground; engineered by the separatists and Pakistan's agents, the propagation of *Wahabi-Islam* by non-Kashmiri religious preachers of *Tablighi-Jamats,* centered in mosques and *Madrasas,* across the length and breadth of the valley, was accentuating; engineered by the separatists and Pakistan's agents, an upheaval in anti-national activities and sloganeering was gaining impetus. The tantrums of unruly mobs, and the encounters between gullible youth, young students in particular, with law and order enforcers, were increasing day by day.

Around 1987, a handful of Indoctrinated Kashmiri Muslim youth, whose conceptions had been cast into the mould of *Jehad* by the separatist elements, were imparted training in guerrilla warfare, including handling and using modern weapons and explosives, in terror training factories of Pakistan, located in POJK. Pakistan had clandestinely started exporting the weapons of death and destruction into the valley to give teeth to prospective terrorists and sponsored saboteurs.

Although majority of Muslims, who lived a tranquil and happy life in the valley, did not support the extremist and separatist elements by subscribing to their ideology of *Jehad*, yet the latter had succeeded in luring a handful of the youth of Kashmir into their fold; and that paved the way for the deadly venomous snake of 'terror' nestling in the valley of Kashmir.

Towards the last quarter of 1988, separatist elements, abetted, aided and supported by Pakistan, caused explosions, using improvised explosive devices and grenades, to terrorize people. Despite a lapse of more than thirty three years, the natives of Srinagar city do reminisce and recall the nightmarish experiences of the IED explosions of July 31, 1988 that rocked the civil lines area of Srinagar. The IED explosions in succession gripped the peace-loving civil society of Kashmir in overwhelming fright as they could read the warning signals, with unmistakable clarity, of the impending disaster.

In the year 1989, nexus between the ideologues of extreme political ideology and remotely controlled terror groups became quite visible in the valley. The bonhomie between terror groups and their underground supporters, cultivated by over-ground protagonists of extreme political ideology, was noticeable; and the features of brazen collusion between the complex political creed of Kashmir and the terror structure were quite comprehensible.

The eruption of terror in Kashmir was not an abrupt phenomenon–it had been 'in-the-making' for years and decades. It can be said with unmistakable clarity that 'Terror in Kashmir' was a measure of the penetration achieved by extremist and separatist elements in creating a broad base for *Jehad*; and what appeared increasingly probable, in an uncertain future, did happen in late 80's.

Separatists were growing in size, and the radical elements were gaining in strength in the peaceful valley. Prospective terrorists were going through radicalization process; and there were visible signs and symptoms of an ugly scenario developing in Kashmir for more than a decade. Arrival of 'Terrorism' was sounding alarm bells, but the political dispensation of India and the state government of J&K were in deep slumber. Both the governments were continually witnessing evil, and doing nothing. The political establishments did not recognize the trouble brewing in the valley of Kashmir even after the horrendous incidents of subversion and sabotage in 1988 and 1989. The manner of dealing with the crisis situation lacked seriousness; and the governments utterly failed to fulfill their constitutional obligations.

What many regarded as most unlikely to materialize did materialize in Kashmir. A numerically small section of Separatists, religious zealots and Pak agents assented to the ideology of gun wielding guerillas. The majority population of the valley chose to remain 'fence-sitters', and that was not for no reason–they didn't want to become the target of gun wielding terrorists, who were desperate and showed no mercy to those becoming an impediment in the way of their scheming.

The terrorists misread the silence of the majority community of Kashmir as tacit approval of their mad acts. They started accelerating the acts of death and destruction, and exhibiting aggressive behavior towards the minuscule minority community members, who they labeled as die-hard nationalists, working as stooges of India in Kashmir.

The inhabitants of the land of *Sufis* and saints knew well that Pakistan was sowing the seeds of discontent and discord in the valley of Kashmir, through its premier intelligence agency, the ISI, and avowed local agents; and they were also quite familiar with all the separatist and political leaders including the religious fanatics, ideologically aligned with Pakistan. Having watched, studied and well grasped the machinations and maneuvers and disruptive behavior of Pakistan since 1947, they, one and all, except the minuscule religious hardliners, who think of Pakistan as their messiah, unhesitatingly and in unequivocal terms say that Pakistan wrecked havoc in Kashmir by abetting, aiding and sponsoring 'terror' that reared its ugly head in late 80's.

Taking advantage of Kashmir's geographical location, Pakistan had been working overtime for about two decades to create an atmosphere of discord, confusion and chaos in the peaceful valley by engaging India in a proxy-war. It succeeded in unleashing a low cost war against India, and the hurricane of violence and terror in J&K claimed more than fifty thousand innocent lives including those swayed in the turbulence; and more than three hundred thousand locals lost their homes and hearths.

With a view to avenging the humiliating defeat of 1971 war that led to Pakistan's disintegration, and formation of Bangladesh, Pakistan had vowed in silent fervor to make India bleed. It wanted to kill two birds with one stone – to disintegrate India and annex Kashmir with it by any means, fair or foul. A secret action plan, Initiated and approved by the then President of Pakistan, General Zia-ul-Haq, had been put in place for action-on-ground.

The salient features of the secret action plan included providing covert funding and logistic support to fringe separatist elements and fundamentalists for triggering unrest and discord in J&K. The action plan emphasized on sowing the seeds of ill-will and hatred against India; spelled-out the mechanism for engineering protests and demonstrations against India; and stressed on luring the youth, students in particular, for causing sabotage and disruption in Kashmir. The intelligence agencies of the whole world know about the sordid and horrendous operation plan of Pakistan, code named 'Operation Tupac'. Alas, the government of India and the political dispensation of the state were in deep slumber.

Pakistan was least afraid in creating a hostile and argumentative situation against mighty India, which was much superior to its military strength, by openly meddling in the affairs of J&K state. This was not for no reason. Pakistan had mastered guerilla warfare techniques. It had engaged the mighty USSR's regular forces in a proxy war, on the soil of Afghanistan in late 70's, in lieu of monetary benefits from the USA. It had gained expertise in running terrorist camps, imparting training to Afghan guerillas, *Jehadis* of other countries and its own country, for fighting against the elite USSR Army. Pakistan had measured and tested its daredevilish skills; and had started believing in its capabilities after the shoddy pull out of USSR from Afghanistan, and its subsequent disintegration.

Pakistan's network comprising its mercenaries and a handful of underground supporters in the valley, sharing Pakistan's ideology, succeeded in silencing the voice of the men of substance and peace-loving majority community members, who exercised considerable influence on Kashmir civil society. The common man erroneously read their silence as an attestation of the situation that was brewing up in the valley; and Pakistan achieved the objective of creating xenophobic phobia in Kashmiri Muslims in the name of *Aazadi* and *Nizam-e-Mustaffa*. Pakistan was emboldened to push more gun wielding guerillas, comprising *Jehadi* fighters and mercenaries, in Kashmir, to open up the theatre of war; and thus, it embarked on the journey of a 'low cost war' against India on the soil of Kashmir.

In January, 1990, terrorists were visible and the government invisible in Kashmir; miniscule minority Hindus were brutally terrorized and battered. Kashmiri Pandits were intimidated, shocked and stunned by Pakistan's mercenaries and their supporters in the valley; and they were left with no option but to flee from their homeland to save their lives, and the honor and dignity of their womenfolk. Not a single voice was raised from anywhere, across the length and breadth of the Kashmir valley, against the outrageous hounding out of the minuscule minority community members from their homeland; and the majority community members of Kashmir civil society became mute spectators to the dreadful onslaught on the centuries-old pluralistic culture and ethos of Kashmir.

Towards the end of 1989, the government of India was led by late V.P Singh, with Mufti Mohammad Sayeed as Home Minister; and the grave and the emergent situation in Kashmir was Soft-pedaled. VP Singh's minority government at the centre, surviving on the clutches of differing political ideologies, looked more concerned about clinging to power than safeguarding the sovereignty and territorial integrity of the country. Both, the state and the central government, failed miserably in protecting and safeguarding the rights of minority Hindus of the valley. Because of political compulsions, the GOI threw up its hands in resignation and helplessness, and utterly failed in effectively dealing with the volatile situation in Kashmir valley. They lay inert in their cozy bungalows in the capital city; and the task of 'Ethnic Cleansing of Kashmir' was accomplished by Pakistan's mercenaries and their supporters.

Despite a lapse of more than thirty two years, the echoes of the horrifying shrieks and spine-chilling sloganeering, simultaneously broadcast on 'Loud Speakers' of various mosques, located in Srinagar city, on the intervening night of January 19-20,1990, continually haunt the miniscule minority community members, the aborigines of Kashmir, to this day. Pre-recorded audio cassettes were used for the purpose; and the content of the warlike high-pitched cries and sloganeering included 'Kashmir *me agar rehna hai, Allah-o-Akbar kehna hai* (if you want to stay in Kashmir, you have to say *Allah-O-Akbar*), and '*Yehan kya chalega, Nizam-e-Mustafa*' (What shall work here, the Rule of *Sharia*); and it was aimed at clutching the miniscule minority members of Kashmiri in extreme fear of impending danger to their lives and property.

With a view to hoodwinking the international community and human rights defenders the world over, Islamic Republic of Pakistan has been croaking like a frog for spreading a fake narrative that it has been providing political, moral and diplomatic support to her co-religionists, followers of '*Quran*', '*Sunnah*' and '*Hadith*' in Kashmir in their so-called struggle for Independence. Some of the selected media outlets, providing News, information and feature stories, on the pay rolls of Pakistan, have been continually spreading downright lies and make-believe stories to conceal Pakistan's sordid machinations; and a section of fundamentalists and bigots, blinded by their sympathetic attitude towards an Islamic country, have been parroting delusive that uprising in Kashmir was indigenous, only to help Pakistan to develop its false narrative.

Truth can't be hidden by falsehood or propaganda for long! Pakistan has been spreading lies and crying wolf to justify her meddling in Indian state of J&K. It has been fomenting trouble and violence in Kashmir for many years, but now, its crafty designs and machinations have petered out. Pakistan is on the radar of the Financial Action Task Force (FATF), a global watchdog for preventing organized crime, money laundering and terrorism; and has been grey-listed in June 2018 for its illegal and crafty actions.

Everybody has his or her reasons for writing and publishing a book. My object of bringing out the myth-busting 'short stories book' is aimed at revealing to the reader the verified true stories, to enable him to take a close look at the machinations and maneuvers of 'war' and 'terror conglomerates' that resulted into the ouster of more than three hundred thousand Kashmiri Hindus from their ancestral land.

Publishing the book titled 'Untold Stories of the Exodus' is my honest effort to give an accurate and authentic account of the true events, happenings and developments which took place in the valley of Kashmir during a particular period.

The stories of displacement of Minority population of Kashmir are not ancient history. The short stories are based on my personal observations and the perennial facts deduced from the real happenings and developments.

The book shall enable the future researchers to know what actually happened in Kashmir; and it shall shake-off the cobwebs of those who were vulnerably exploited by false narratives and misguided religious appeal.

The verified 'real short stories' shall bring to fore hitherto some of the unknown facts about why and how the abode of humanistic traditions of great Sufis and saints was engulfed in 'terror', leading to death, destruction and ethnic cleansing; and it shall help the reader to discover the intent, design and the origin of violence and disorder in the valley. Two of the Short stories of the book unfold in most unequivocal terms the machinations of Pakistan for causing death and destruction in the peaceful valley of Kashmir with the active support of the forces of mayhem and the villains of peace.

The book is a collection of verified real stories, based on actual events, with fictitious names, characters and places; and any resemblance to actual persons, living or dead, is purely coincidental.

> *"When the conscience runs pure and strong in the heart of thinking humanity, there is no power in any fundamentalism to take hold of the human civilization and drag it back to the medieval days of barbarism."*
>
> **– Abhijit Naskar**

1

Pakistan's Maneuvers To Besiege *Kashmiriyat*

(June, 1985)

It was a mid-summer day in 1985. The Sun was inching to dip below the horizon; the scintillating effects of the pre-sun-set over the soft blue haze of *Dal-Lake* were mesmeric; and the happy *bulbuls* were disporting themselves in and around the flower gardens of *Cheshma-Shahi*, Nishat and Shalimar! A fair-complexioned non-local tourist, apparently looking in the mid 30's, in the company of a local youth, appeared on the hill-top near the *Shankaracharya* temple. Below the logo of *Khel-Bharti* on the embroidered crest of the blue blazer he was wearing, a 7-letter word in English, 'Shakeel', clearly indicated his name.

Infatuated with the passion of flowers and the greenery of highlands, Shakeel mounted his camera on a tripod, and busied himself in taking pictures of the panoramic view of magnificent Chinar trees, somnolent looking River Jhelum, and artistic layout of the house-boats, plazas and dwelling houses. The enchanting beauty of the land filled him with a mad longing; and with each capturing of a picture, the joyful words '*Masha-Allah*', poured out of his mouth.

After sundown, the daylight was fading fast; the chirping birds were retreating to their roosts; and young football players, toiling in the pompous Amarsingh College campus of Srinagar also left, one by one, except for a group of six. The group eagerly waited for the arrival of their fellow-footballer, who was scheduled to come along with a non-local, running an NGO for the promotion of football.

Hameed and Shakeel reached Amar Singh College campus with a cardboard box containing gift packets of football-jerseys, shoes and footballs; and the group members greeted Shakeel warmly. They wished him in Muslim tradition as they had been told by their fellow footballer, Hameed, that Shakeel was a Muslim from Maler-kotla, Punjab. In his brief self-introduction, he smilingly said, "I am the Chief patron of *Khel Bharti*, an NGO, engaged in promotion of football; my close acquaintances fondly call me by the name 'Triple-S'; and the three Ss denotes 'Sports-Sportsman-Shakeel'; and my name is Shakeel".

He presented a gift packet each to seven footballers including Hameed. The recipients of the gift-packs expressed their words of gratitude, and Shakeel said, "All praise is to *Allah*; I am grounded in the firm belief that blessed are the Muslims who dedicate themselves to the welfare of their Muslim-brethren world over; and I have devoted my life to a noble cause."

After a few minutes, Shakeel said to Hameed, "Hameed *Bhai*, I think we must leave now, it is already late; let's hope to meet at 'Prang' tomorrow, if *Allah* wills; and it shall be a divine opportunity for all of us to converse informally." Both left in an auto-rickshaw to Magarmal Bagh area where a hotel room had already been booked for his stay.

Son of a well-to-do businessmen and mainstream politician, Hameed, a college drop-out in his mid 20's, was a resident of the civil lines area of Srinagar. Inspired by the football legends, Christiano Ronald and Diego Maradona, he spent most of his time playing football.

From his teen age, Hameed had a strong desire to acquire thorough knowledge about *Islam*, its reverences, essentials and obligations; and he regularly visited a Mosque in the civil lines area of Srinagar to hear the religious sermons of a non-local *Maulvi* for many years. Sermons of the *Maulvi* brought about a change in his outlook on life; he got firmly fixed in the belief that the peace, tranquility and brotherhood could only be brought through *Nizam-e-Mustafa,* the rule of Sharia; and he stood for achieving the universal sovereignty of *Allah* and *Islam*. He had started sporting beard, donning a white skull cap and wearing the trouser slightly above the ankle. A year ago, on the occasion of *Shab-e-Baraat,* Hameed had met and interacted with Shakeel for the first time in the precincts of a Mosque.

Hameed wanted to solicit feedback from Shakeel about his introductory meeting with the group of footballers on Amarsingh college campus; and immediately after entering the Hotel room, he said to Shakeel, "Sir; are you satisfied?"

"Hameed *Bhai*, it was just the beginning of what we have got our sights set on; I am satisfied, but it was not something extraordinary, worthy of celebration; and we have to work hard tirelessly." Shakeel replied, with a smile.

"Yes, we have to."

"I want you to keep me updated on the progress of your efforts and developments in Kashmir, truthfully and accurately." Shakeel said, smilingly.

"Shakeel *Bhai*, I shall be a sinner if ever I give you a painted or exaggerated picture of my efforts or ground realities, just to please you; and I swear by Allah that I shall be always veracious, even if it hurts you." Hameed replied.

"Hameed *Bhai*, I know that you are a true Muslim; and you will never mislead me by lying." Shakeel said, with a smile.

"Yes, Certainly; I shall never do that."

"I can understand that." Shakeel said.

"Shakeel *Bhai*, although I have been working hard tirelessly, yet I am dismayed to see a limited appeal in my discourses with the people I met; and It took me more than two months to impress and shut off only a handful of Kashmiri youth from their deep-rooted belief." Hameed said, with a sigh of disgust.

"Belief; which belief are you talking about?" Shakeel asked.

"Shakeel *Bhai*, Kashmiri Muslims are the followers of Sufis, saints and worshipers of shrines and tombs; and this is true of even those who think of themselves as 'devout Muslims'. The psyche of Kashmiri Muslims is deeply rooted in *Kashmiriyat*– a peculiar pluralistic ethos and secular ideology." Hameed said, with a sigh of disappointment.

"Don't they desire to become part of Islamic Republic of Pakistan?" Shakeel asked inquisitively.

"Honestly speaking, if given a choice, Kashmiri Muslims would choose independence; and if they were to decide between India and Pakistan, I think, Kashmiri Muslims shall choose India. My opinion is based on my personal assessment, I may be wrong." Hameed replied, with a smile.

"Why would Kashmiri Muslims choose India, if given a choice to be with Islamic Republic of Pakistan?" Shakeel asked.

"Shakeel *Bhai*, the state of J&K has been inhabited by distinct ethnic and linguistic groups for centuries; the people of Kashmir have a unique and distinct historical and cultural background; and history bears testimony that Kashmiri Muslims had strongly opposed the idea of the partition of united India on religious lines." Hameed replied emphatically.

"True; Please tell me, why?" Shakeel asked.

"Perhaps, Kashmiris wanted Kashmir to remain independent of India and Pakistan, both." Hameed replied, shaking his head in disgust.

"Do you mean to say that Kashmiri Muslims have a feeling of ill will against Islamic republic of Pakistan; and they don't appreciate that Pakistan has been fully supporting the Independence movement of Kashmir for the last 38 years?" Shakeel asked, inquisitively.

"Shakeel B*hai*, according to my assessment and analysis, a section of Kashmiri Muslims, numerically small though, has intense and passionate feeling for Pakistan because they long to see the whole world run by 'Nizam-*e-Mustaffa*, but the majority population of Kashmiri Muslims doesn't show any special interest for Pakistan."

"Why?" Shakeel asked instantly.

"Kashmiri Muslims are grounded in the belief that after the division of India and fragmentation of Kashmir in 1947, Muslims in Kashmir and other parts of India have been living happily, with rights protected and secured; and Kashmiri Muslims have a false notion that they prospered and bloomed much better than the people living in the areas of Kashmir occupied by Pakistan." Hameed replied unhesitatingly, with a deep sigh.

"Are Kashmiris namesake Muslims; are they averse to the ideology of global Islamisation?" Shakeel asked.

"No, sir; Kashmiri Muslims firmly believe in the teachings of Quran and the *Sharia*; they are neither insincere to Pakistan nor averse to the globalization of Islam." Hameed said forcefully.

"That is good News. Now, tell me honestly, why Kashmiris don't want to be part of Islamic Republic of Pakistan?" Shakeel asked.

"In my opinion, *Kashmiriyat* is firmly entrenched in the minds of Kashmiri Muslims, and they fear that if Kashmir is annexed by Islamic Republic of Pakistan, civilizational conflicts and divisions in the name of religion shall engulf the entire J&K state, and that shall lead to further fragmentation of the state." Hameed said.

Don't you think that the stupid psyche of Kashmiri Muslims needs complete overhauling?

"Shakeel B*hai*, yes; they do behave in stupid ways. They have retained many unwanted things from their heritage; their minds are impacted by the faiths and cultures of Buddhists, Brahmins and Jews; they have institutionalized a symbiotic fusion with the people believing in non-sense practices, and they follow many of their traditions, customs and rituals. I say this without any inhibition or reservation, because you told me to be honest in my revelations". Hameed said.

Niggled Shakeel took a deep sigh and murmured–"*Kashmiriyat.*" He looked at the wall-clock; hurriedly got up from the chair, and told Hameed that he had to visit Lal Chowk area to arrange transport and food etc for the scheduled picnic; and both left the hotel room in haste.

Next day, as already planned, Hameed and the group of six football players, were conducted by Shakeel, in a chartered passenger van, to Prang, a famous picnic spot enroute to Sonamarg, located on the outskirts of Srinagar city along the River Indus. After serving them a sumptuous break-fast, Shakeel started interaction with all.

Rashid, a member of the group, pursuing his post graduation degree at Kashmir University, in reply to a query by Shakeel, said in a harsh tone, "Yes; Pakistan has been confusing the 'movement of *Azadi*' of Kashmiris for the last 38 years."

Rashid's reaction provoked Shakeel, and he asked: "Are you a Muslim or a Kashmiri Brahmin?"

"Shakeel sahib, please don't get excited without any reason; and don't use contemptuous words." Rashid said angrily.

Furrowing his eyebrows, Shakeel said, "Please tone down."

"Shakeel sahib, you must remember that a true Muslim never arrogates himself to the position of infallibility and perfection." Rashid said, with a sullen face.

Observing the body language and the facial expressions of Hameed, Shakeel instantly said, "Rashid *Bhai*, I think that my words have hurt you, I am sorry."

"Take it easy, Shakeel Bhai" Rashid replied, smilingly.

"We were talking about the 'movement of *Azadi*', please carry on." Shakeel said, looking deep into Rashid's eyes.

"Shakeel *Bhai*, I reiterate that Pakistan has been concentrating on her own advantage right since her birth in 1947; with the sole object of extending its territories, Pakistan has been tricking Kashmiri Muslims; and its claim of supporting Kashmiri Muslims is nothing but humbug." Rashid said, vehemently.

"Rashid *Bhai*, the entire Islamic world regards Islamic Republic of Pakistan with respect and admiration, and you are talking nonsense by spitting venom against Pakistan."Shakeel thundered at Rashid, angrily.

Shaklee's terse reply angered Rashid, and despite intervention by Hameed and other members to pacify him, enraged Rashid left in protest. While leaving, he said to Shakeel, "Islam is the religion of peace, brotherhood and harmony; and Pakistan has not been mandated by the Muslims world over to meddle in the personal affairs of Muslims for fulfilling her political agenda."

Hameed followed the angry Rashid; used his acquiescent skills to back him off from his decision of leaving unceremoniously. He succeeded in making Rashid shun the acrimonious feelings; and Rashid rejoined.

Members of the group had a sumptuous lunch; and spent the day together in the company of their host, Shakeel. While leaving the picnic spot in the evening, Shakeel, in an emotional outburst with tearful eyes, addressed the group members. "My dear brothers; we are all believers; the signs from the soul come silently; you need to respond to them authentically; and I assure you that one day we will win the world!" Shakeel said.

As a token of love, he presented Rupees ten thousand each, to all of them, as gift, which they accepted smilingly.

Shakeel was on a covert mission, even his close associate, Hameed, could not comprehend initially. He wanted to rope in youth of Kashmir to portray the view of radical Islamists to galvanize frenzy against *Kashmiriyat*. At the instance of Shakeel, Hameed had founded 'Falcon football Club' in Srinagar, and the former provided him liberal funding for running the club. He regularly paid handsome pocket money to Hameed, and to his other club members, through him. Gradually, Hameed became his indispensable asset in the valley of Kashmir for accomplishing impious activities in a secret manner.

Energized by the Hameed's resourcefulness, bold initiatives, eloquence to win over youth and feedback on his performance, Shakeel started trusting him with major responsibilities. Accompanying Shakeel, Hameed travelled to

Pakistan also, via Nepal, for a short four day visit, on a fake passport and false documents, provided to him by the former.

Hameed's quiet demeanor and persona were deceptive; he was not a gullible young man. He had the ability to learn, understand and to deal with difficult situations. Shaklee's loyalty and strong feelings of support for Pakistan and his lavish spending of money had led him to believe that Shakeel was acting at the behest of Pakistan. He had even confided this to his cousin, Maqbool.

'Time' and 'life' were moving on like the River Jhelum and other streams in the valley of Kashmir, which apparently looked peaceful. Shakeel was busy accomplishing the 'Mission' in dramatic and surprising ways; and he paid frequent visits to Srinagar to hold meetings with Hameed and other indoctrinated youth, in the guise of football promoter.

(May, 1986)

In May, 1986, Hameed met Shakeel in Nehru Park area of Srinagar city. In the course of the meeting, Shakeel opened his heart, and said, "Hameed, I have grasped it well that Kashmiri Muslims have embraced an indigenous life-style which does not conform to the teachings of Quran and *Sharia*; they do not identify themselves with other Muslims of the world, because they are wedded to irreligious rituals and practices; and *Kashmiriyat* is a stumbling block in envisioning and enforcing *Nizam-e-Mustafa* in Kashmir."

"Shakeel *Bhai*, that's what I have been telling you from day one." Hameed replied instantly.

"Is it not essential to demolish the structure of *Kashmiriyat,* and pile its bits into a heap? Shakeel said.

"Shakeel Bhai, yes; and we need to do that!" Hameed replied.

"Hameed *Bhai*, tell me how?" Shakeel said instantly.

Hameed stood dumb as he was clueless about the method to be adopted, and his senses were numb.

Shakeel was on a hunt to lure and entice more people of the valley to work for him. He wanted to widen the ambit of his activities by roping in students of Kashmir University; and bore in mind that Hameed's two first cousins were studying at Kashmir University.

Shakeel asked Hameed to arrange his meeting with a non-local *Maulvi,* namely *Maulvi* Ramzan, his operative in the valley. Hameed innocently assented, and a luncheon outing was planned for sharing of thoughts and ideas with Maulvi Ramzan; and Shakeel asked Hameed to invite his two first cousins for joining the outing.

As planned, Shakeel, accompanied by a non local, reached near the embankment of a stream in Dachigam area, in the outskirts of Srinagar city, half an hour before the scheduled meeting, and rolled out a carpet on a patch of green turf to sit on. Within a few minutes *Maulvi*, Hameed and his two cousins also reached there. Hameed introduced the *Maulvi* as Ramzan, a native of Bareli, UP, and the other two as Maqbool and Fayaz, his cousins, both pursuing post- graduation courses; and Shakeel introduced the middle-aged non local as Mudasar, a native of Maler-kotla, Punjab.

After exchanging pleasantries, Shakeel got down to business by initiating a discourse with *Maulvi* Ramzan, as if he didn't know him, and said, "*Maulvi* sahib, you are an Islamic scholar, an authority on religious matters; kindly enlighten me about your views on *Kashmiriyat*."

"Kashmiriyat is humbug; a true Muslim is bound to follow the *Quran* and *Sharia*; and anybody who follows and abides by any other ideology is Kafir." *Maulvi* Ramzan replied.

"Can *Kafir* become a friend of Muslims?" Shakeel asked.

"*Kafir* is a liar, stumbling in the depths of ignorance; and a believer must never befriend *Kafir* in preference to a believer." *Maulvi* Ramzan replied.

"What about the people who claim to be Islamists to the core, but propagate and nurture *Kashmiriyat?"* Shakeel asked.

"Shakeel *Bhai*, *Kashmiriyat* is not in conformity with the ideology of Islam; I call them hypocrites; and they fall in the category of *Kafirs."* Maulvi replied.

"How should a Muslim deal with *Kafir*?" Shakeel asked.

"There is no change in the ways of *Allah*: *Kafirs* will be cursed; they should be hounded out of the land; and if you don't do that, they shall create problems for you." Maulvi Ramzan replied.

It took Maqbool no time to grasp that Maulvi Raman's quizzing by Shakeel was not intended to obtain or gain knowledge about Islamic affairs, but to tease him and two other Kashmiri Muslims present there. He was prompted to join the discourse, and, with utmost humility, he said to *Maulvi*, "*Maulana* sahib, if you permit me, I would like to share my perception on the subject". Directing his eyes swiftly towards the sky, Maulvi replied, hesitatingly though, "Please go ahead."

"According to my knowledge, the word '*Kafir*' denotes a 'non believer' in Islamic revelations; and Muslims have to be kind and just to non-believers, except those who actively fight and unjustly expel believers from their homes." Maqbool said.

After a covert gaze on his face, *Maulvi* Ramzan said, "Are you a Muslim?"

Maqbool grasped well that *Maulvi* did not like his reply. Yet again, in a sober tone, he said, "Maulana sahib, *Allah* is my God; Prophet Mohammad is my savior; and holy *Quran* is my guide".

Maqbool's reply irritated Maulvi further; and he sarcastically said, "Have you read Quran?"

Maqbool instantly said, "Maulana sahib, by the grace of *Allah*, I have read holy *Quran* and its commentaries by widely and highly honored Islamic scholars, not once but umpteen times; and I may inform you that I have memorized all the chapters of the Holly *Quran*, and you can test me.

"Maulvi was astonished to hear the instant reply, and he clumsily said, "I reiterate that *Kashmiriyat* does not conform to teachings of Islam."

"Maulana sahib, *Kashmiriyat* has been a style of serene life for Kashmiri Muslims for centuries; and I fail to understand how *Kashmiriyat* is un-Islamic?" Maqbool replied.

Maqbool's words provoked Maulvi to anger, and he said, "*Kashmiriyat* is '*Kufr*'; the command of Allah for Muslims is to follow the *Quran* and *Sharia* only; and, therefore, all those following the ideology of *Kashmiriyat* are sinners."

"Kashmiriyat is a way of life, not a religious faith; the concrete foundations of '*Kashmiriyat*' in Kashmir have been laid by *Sultan-ul-Aarifeen*, *Sheikh-ul-Aalam*, *Amir-e-Kabir*, Bulbul Shah and others; for centuries, the Kashmiris bloomed and prospered, in an atmosphere of peace and tranquility by adapting the inspirational and unique way of life." Maqbool said to Maulvi.

Maqbools's words discomposed Maulvi, and he reacted in a fit of anger: "You appear to me a '*Brahman-zada*', the progeny of *Brahmans*."

Hearing this, gravely provoked Maqbool yelled at Maulana, "Yes; I am the proud progeny of *Brahmans*, the aborigines of Kashmir, who allowed unobstructed and smooth propagation of Buddhism and Islam in their land; and my ancestors have embraced Islam, not by forcible conquest but by hassle-free conversion. History bears the testimony that never

ever did my ancestors start a campaign of hatred and intolerance against those who among them embraced Islam. For your kind information, my ancestors have a continued history from the age of pit and cave dwellers to the present."

Hot-headed Maulana lost his composure and brawled, "You are talking shit; I can understand that you are a superficially altered person."

Maqbool lost the ability to control his hurt feelings and said, "O' illiterate Maulvi, What do you mean by saying '*superficially altered person*'?"

"Through your words and actions, you are carrying forward the narrative of *Kafirs*; in doing that, you are becoming the partner of *Satan;* you are propagating a distorted version of the Islam beyond measure; and I have no reservation in declaring you 'unclean'. Embittered Maulana said to Maqbool.

Maqbool camouflaged his sentiments with a fake smile; and satirically said to Maulvi, "Maulana sahib, you are a learned religious scholar; please guide us on what we, the Kashmiri Muslims, need to do?"

Maulvi mistook his satire as surrender, and said, "*Kashmiriyat* is Kufr, and all those propagating *Kufr* are *Kafirs*, worthy of annihilation; *Kafirs* deserve to be disgraced, crucified and terrorized; they should be hounded out without showing any feeling of sorrow and sympathy; and you need to do that."

The heated arguments between the *Maulvi* Ramzan and Maqbool continued for some time; after yelling, both started exchanging invectives of the worst kind at each other; and, in the spur of moment, a violent scuffle ensued between the two.

Maqbool, Fayaz and Hameed severely thrashed Maulana and Shakeel; pushed both of them into the stream; and consigned the food containers, accoutrements and personal belongings of Maulvi and Shakeel into the gushing water of the stream.

Angry Maqbool, Hammed and Fayaz left the place. Rude and antisocial attitude and behavior displayed by *Maulvi* Ramzan towards his cousin, Maqbool, had caused a lot of hurt feelings to Hameed, and *Maulvi's* provocative and contemptuous words *'Brahman-zada'*, 'talking shit' and 'superficially altered person' haunted him. He yelled at the fleeing trio, "O' you, megalomaniac, stupid people; go and tell your master-minds and sponsors that intelligent Kashmiri Muslims are neither going to get carried away nor won over by falsehood; convey to them that Kashmiris are firmly grounded in the belief that humanity and peace are the fundamentals of Islam, and they refuse to buy misinterpreted and irrational concept of religion."

After they fled from the spot, Maulvi Ramzan and Shakeel were never seen in the valley!

> *"Spies are, by nature and necessity, pathological liars who strive to make their endgames justify their meanness."*
>
> **– Stewart Stafford**

2

Pakistan's Machinations For Ethnic Cleansing

(April, 13, 1988)

With the advent of spring in Kashmir valley, the view of the blooming almond, cherry, peach and apple trees was simply gorgeous, and watching the landscape of the valley from a distance was a feast for the eyes; and the robust sweet aroma of the almond blossoms was aesthetically pleasing. The tourists, both domestic and foreign, were making a beeline at various inter-state bus terminals and airports in India to visit Kashmir.

On the afternoon of April, 13, 1988, Solar New Year day, called *Baisakhi*, Shamsher Singh and Iqbal Singh, both foreign nationals, were on board an aircraft of Indian Airlines that touched-down at the Srinagar Airport. They had entered India on tourist visas, and their destination was *Chatti Padshahi* Gurduwara, located in the Kathi-darwaza area of Rainawari, Srinagar.

Hindus celebrate the descent of Goddess Ganga on this day. The day marks the Sikh New Year, and commemorates the formation of '*Khalsa Panth*'. *Chatti Padshahi* Gurdwara, the central place of worship for Sikhs in Kashmir, is believed to have been constructed by the sixth Sikh Guru, Shri Hargobind Singh Ji, and his ardent devotee *Mayi* Bhagbhari. The Gurdwara is situated outside the Hari-Parbat fort's southern gate in Srinagar.

Haji Yusuf Dar, a native of Srinagar, engaged in tourism-trade in Kashmir valley, reached the Srinagar airport, an hour before the scheduled time of the arrival of the flight– to pick up Shamsher Singh and Iqbal Singh. Holding placards in their hands, with words written in bold letters–'Shamsher Singh and Iqbal Singh–our pleasure to receive you at the Airport–Welcome', Haji Yusuf Dar and the car driver, Liyakat Ali, positioned themselves near the exit gate of the arrival lounge.

Sporting an untrimmed beard, attired in Punjabi style *Kurta* and *pyjama*, and wearing typical Sikh turban, differentiated the duo from other passengers. After the guests exited, Haji Yusuf Dar greeted them in Sikh tradition '*Sat Shri Akal*', and the guests, with a meaningful smile, reciprocated the wish. The friendly reception of Haji Yusuf Dar was no less pleasant and enjoyable for the guests than the springtime weather and blossoming of almond trees in Kashmir.

The guests boarded the car, and reached *Chatti Padshahi Gurdwara* within half an hour. After joining the recitation of *Gurubani,* and paying obeisance to the holy book of the Sikhs, Sri Guru Granth Sahib, Haji Yusuf Dar transported them to his residence cum tourist guest-house, located in the posh civil lines area of Srinagar city. While entering the well-fenced residence cum tourist guest-house, Haji Yusuf Dar instructed the security guard not to allow anybody, not even his friends and relatives, to enter without his permission. After taking light refreshments, the guests spent the rest of the day on the green lawns of the guest house under a canopy.

At around 9 pm, while Haji Yusuf Dar was personally supervising the preparation of Kashmiri cuisine, the *Wazwan*, in the Kitchen room, his 5-year old son, Riyaz, came running and said to his father, Haji Yusuf Dar, "*Papa*, *Papa*, do the 'Sikhs' offer *Namaz* as Muslmans do?"

Not knowing the exact reason for the query, Haji Yusuf Dar instantly said, "No".

"*Papa,* you say that Sikhs don't offer *Namaz*, but the Sikh guests have replaced their turbans with Muslim caps, and are busy offering *Namaz* over the rolled out prayer-mats on the floor of the room." Little Riyaz said to his father innocently.

The reasoning and analytical abilities of little Riyaz, and his power of observation stunned Haji Yusuf Dar. He knew well that the guests were Shamsher Khan and Iqbal Cheema, both Punjabi speaking Muslims from Pakistani, in the guise of Sikhs, but he said to Riyaz, "The two Sikh guests have already checked out, and two Muslim guests have checked in."

The guests were served a sumptuous *Kashmiri Wazwan* at around 10 pm, and while the chef, two waiters and the young Riyaz were around, Haji Yusuf Dar addressed the guests as 'Shamsher *Bhai*' and 'Iqbal *Bhai*' repeatedly, and not Shamsher Singh and Iqbal Singh. Observing the guests minutely near the dining table, little Riyaz quietly said to his father into his ear, "*Papa*, the guests are wearing the similar embroidered footwear as the Sikh guests had worn during the day." The words astounded and enraged Haji Yusuf Dar; and to shut Riyaz's mouth, he gave him a fierce reprimand to stop talking superfluous.

After dinner, the guests had a close-door long conversation with Haji Yusuf Dar until midnight. Before retiring to their beds in the adjoining bedroom, Shamsher Khan contacted one Bilal Ahmad, a native of the down-town area, telephonically, and asked him to come to the guest house, along with his two friends at 10 am, the next day; and Haji Yusuf Dar, after wishing the guests in the Islamic tradition, left well after midnight.

(April, 14, 1988)

On the morning of April, 14, 1988, after scheduling their activities for the day, Shamsher Khan and Iqbal Cheema started a leisurely walk in the garden of the guesthouse to enjoy the pleasant weather, sun-rise and the sights of breathtaking views of the snow-capped mountains.

Shamsher Khan and Iqbal Cheema wanted to have a hair-cut and trim their long beard; and Haji Yusuf Dar called a barber to the guesthouse. After the barber did his job, they got attired in typical Kashmiri Muslim dress.

At 10 am sharp, the gatekeeper of the Guest House walked in, and informed Haji Yusuf Dar about the arrival of Bilal Ahmad, Ayub and Mushtaq. Shamsher Khan and Iqbal Cheema exchanged looks at Haji Yusuf Dar with a smile, and the latter asked the gatekeeper to allow them in; and he further told him not to allow anybody in without his permission. Nodding his head, the gatekeeper left, and the group of three entered in.

The trio walked straight into the drawing-room, they offered Islamic standard salutation "*Assalam alaykum Warahmatullah Wabarakatuh.*" to Haji Yusuf Dar and the guests. The invitees were greeted in traditional Islamic style "*Walaykum Assalam*" in unison, and, demonstrating affection and emotional warmth, Haji Yusuf Dar and the guests hugged them, one by one.

Driven by the ideology of bringing the whole world under *Nizam-e-Mustafa*, with Islamic Republic of Pakistan as their source of ideology, the invitees remained actively engaged in discussing the broader aspects of socio-political situation of Kashmir for quite some time. With a view to keeping Shamsher Khan and Iqbal Cheema in good humor, the trio, one after another, praised Pakistan for discharging its obligation as messiah of Muslims world over. Emotionally charged Bilal Ahmed, with tearful eyes, said to Shamsher Khan, "Shamsher B*hai*, I am aware of the fact that I am not permitted to bow to anybody except the *Allah*, but if I were permitted, I would bow my head to you!"

"Why?" Shamsher Khan asked, gazing at the tearful eyes of Bilal Ahmed.

"Shamsher *Bhai*, I see a true *Musalman* in you; and you are working earnestly for *Nizam-e-Mustaffa.*" Bilal Ahmed replied, with a smile.

"That is *Allah's* will! I am getting the unflinching support of devoted Muslims like you." Shamsher Khan replied, looking up towards the ceiling of the room.

"Shamsher *Bhai*, I have once and for all pledged my support for the Islamic campaign you have started, and I shall long to do that." Bilal Ahmed said to Shamsher Khan, gazing at his face.

"I consider myself a '*Sipahi*', a soldier of 'Islam'." Shamsher Khan replied.

"Shamsher *Bhai*, you are a senior-rank officer of Pakistan's Field Intelligence Unit, the FIU, but even then, you consider yourself a '*Sipahi*'– I must say that you are down to earth, free from pride, arrogance and ego; you listen to the others patiently; and speak your mind clearly without any inhibition." Bilal Ahmed replied with a smile.

"Who told you that I am from FIU?" Shamsher Khan asked, with an intent look at Bilal's face.

"Shamsher Khan Sahib, you used to pay regular visits to our training camp to ensure our welfare; and I remember the day well when you escorted me and six other Kashmiri *Mujahedeen*, from Athumuqam training Camp of Azad Kashmir to Pakistan border post for exfilitration." Bilal Ahmed replied-with twinkling bright eyes.

Bilal Ahmad's straightforwardness and words of admiration radiated positive feelings and happiness to Shamsher Khan and Iqbal Cheema, and both gazed at his face with a smile.

The Interaction between Bilal Ahmed and the guests continued; and Haji Yusuf Dar remained engrossed in analyzing their words and thoughts.

Haji Yusuf Dar had been working as an agent of Pakistan's Secret Service Intelligence agency, ISI, in the valley of Kashmir, for quite some time, and he had the knowledge that Bilal Ahmed had received the training in handling and using of weapons and explosives in a training camp located in Pakistan Occupied Kashmir (POK), but had no inkling of the fact that Ayub and Mushtaq had also received the training in the same camp.

While Bilal Ahmad started making some candid revelations about the Athumuqam Training camp in the presence of Ayub and Mushtaq, Haji Yusuf made a grimacing face. He panned his surprising looks simultaneously at the faces of the guests including Bilal Ahmed, and quietly said to Bilal into his ear, "Please don't you go off-limits."

Although Shamsher Khan conveyed to Haji Yusuf Dar, through the motion of his hands and eyes, with a smile, that Ayub and Mushtaq were Bilal Ahmad's training mates, yet he could not comprehend that; and he heaved a sigh of relief only after Shamsher Khan said, "Ayub *Bhai* and Mushtaq *Bhai* are among my trusted assets in the valley of Kashmir."

The conversation between Shamsher Khan and Iqbal Cheema with three invitees continued for more than two hours. The trio reiterated their commitment that they were ready to fight; and lay down their lives for achieving the shared goal of the Muslims of Pakistan and Kashmir– to secede Kashmir from India!

Before giving Bilal Ahmad, Ayub and Mushtaq a send off from the guest house, they were served Wazwan, a Kashmiri cuisine; and, in recognition of their selfless service of *Ummat al-Islam*, Shamsher Khan presented to them Rupees one lakh each in Indian currency, as reward money, which they accepted gladly.

After the trio left, Haji Yusuf Dar conducted Shamsher Khan and Iqbal Cheema to a houseboat in Nageen Lake area of Srinagar for a closed-door meeting with Mohammad Anwar and Abdul Aziz, both residents of Srinagar's downtown area.

Mohammad Anwar, a staunch religious zealot, was a die-hard votary of seceding J&K from India and uniting it with Pakistan; and Abdul Aziz advocated complete political freedom of united Kashmir, the area administered by India and the area under the occupation of Pakistan. Although their political ideologies were poles apart yet both had a common object–to change the political system of the state of J&K.

After their post graduation from Kashmir University in 'History' and 'Political Science' respectively, Mohammad Anwar and Abdul Aziz were lured by Pakistan's agents, active in the valley, to carry forward their agenda of seceding Kashmir from India. They had been trained in guerilla warfare and subversion in one of the trainings camps of Pakistan, a few months ago; and the brain-washed academicians had set out on their journey to incite people to rebellion in the valley of Kashmir.

Shamsher Khan and Iqbal Cheema were on a 'Mission'! Iqbal Cheema had interacted with Mohammad Anwar and Abdul Aziz, during their training, in one of the terrorist training camps of Pakistan. In one of his meetings, Iqbal Cheema had confided to Shamsher khan that among all the *Mujahedeen* from Kashmir, Mohammad Anwar and Abdul Aziz were daredevils with natural instincts of hunting lions. Shamsher Khan and Iqbal Cheema knew well that they exercised a strong influence on the youth of Kashmir, and regarded both as potent guerrillas.

Initiating the conversation, Shamsher Khan touched their emotionally ailing nerve by emphasizing that Pakistan, an Islamic Republic, has been earnestly working to spread *Nizam-e-Mustaffa* globally, but India's occupation of Kashmir was the biggest impediment in achieving that. This prompted Mohammad Anwar to open up and he said to Shamsher Khan, "Sir, India regards Kashmir as its colony, and bullies Kashmiris in the manner English did to the citizens of united India before Independence."

"Yes, India has been doing that since 1947." Shamsher Khan replied.

"Shamsher B*hai*, a section of Kashmiri Muslims hope that Kashmir shall become an independent sovereign country. Is that possible?" Mohammad Anwar asked anxiously.

"Anwar B*hai,* that is not achievable; all those who think that Kashmir shall become an 'Independent country' are crazy; and I call them day-dreamers." Shamsher Khan replied bluntly.

"Why does Pakistan cry aloud that it is supporting the 'freedom movement of Kashmiri Muslims?" Mohammad Anwar asked curiously.

"Anwar B*hai*, if we call 'Kashmiri Wazwan' by any other name, will it lose grandeur and the taste?" Shamsher Khan replied, with a smile.

"Shamsher Khan *Bhai*, I could not understand the symbolic meaning, please elaborate" Mohammad Anwar asked anxiously.

"Anwar B*hai*, Pakistan recognizes the right of self-determination of Kashmiri Muslims. According to the UN resolutions, the only two options available to Kashmiris are to choose between India and Pakistan, and there is no option of

'*Azadi*' in UN resolutions. Pakistan has been openly extending moral, political and diplomatic support to Kashmiri Muslims; it has devised a well thought strategic plan; and it wants to end the subjugation of Kashmiri Muslims at any cost. Pakistan and Kashmiri Muslims have a shared goal, and both need to stand shoulder to shoulder with each other." Shamsher Khan replied.

"I want you to be candid in what exactly you mean by standing 'shoulder to shoulder' with each other, and what Kashmiri Muslims need to do?" Mohammad Anwar asked innocently.

"You are a student of History; and you must have read that the Indian Army chased the tribals and invaders up to Domel in Uri sector in 1947, and then abruptly called off the operation even when there was no resistance from Pakistan Army regulars and the tribals." Shamsher Khan replied, with a gaze on Mohammad Anwar's face.

"Yes, that was astonishing!" Mohammad Anwar replied.

"Do you know the reason for that?" Shamsher Khan asked, arching his eyebrows.

"I have never pondered over that." Mohammad Anwar replied.

"Anwar B*hai*, it was only because the Kotli, Muzaffarabad and other areas had been made free of Hindus, they were either killed or forced to flee by the raiders. A Hindu dominated country was not interested in reclaiming the captured areas which were inhabited by not even a single Hindu." Shamsher Khan replied, looking into the eyes of Mohammad Anwar with a meaningful smile.

"Shamsher B*hai*, there is logic in what you say." Mohammad Anwar said.

"I never talk for talking sake" Shamsher Khan said, smilingly.

"Anwar B*hai*, you know that Pakistan, an Islamic country, is engaged in fostering global Islamisation. It wants the 'believers of Islam', world over, to discharge the religious obligation of extending full support to Pakistan for achieving the goal–and the time has come for the submitters to *Allah* from Kashmir to contribute their mite in the service of Islam." Shamsher Khan said with a smile.

Abdul Aziz was observing quietly; and he chose to stay silent. His body language suggested that Shamsher Khan was talking rationale and logic. Highly impressed by the opinion and beliefs of Shamsher Khan, Abdul Aziz broke the silence by joining the discussion. Expressing his readiness to do everything in the service of Islam, he said to Shamsher Khan, "Shamsher Bhai, please tell me what exactly you want Kashmiri Muslims to do?"

"Aziz B*hai*, you know well that area-wise and population-wise, India is much bigger than Pakistan; and we can succeed only if we jointly make India bleed with a thousand cuts." Shamsher Khan replied, with a glow of lust in his eyes.

"Shamsher *Bhai*, How can we do that?" Abdul Aziz asked.

"Aziz B*hai*, together we can start a covert war against India for achieving the common goal." Shamsher Khan replied, with a smile.

"What shall be the role of Kashmiri Muslims?" Abdul Aziz asked.

"Kashmiri Muslims shall have to prepare the ground for Pakistan's direct military confrontation with Indian Army in Kashmir." Shamsher Khan replied, waving his arms in the air.

"How shall we do that?" Abdul Aziz asked, innocently.

"Aziz *Bhai*, first of all, you shall have to hound out *Kafirs* from Kashmir. You shall have to force them to leave; intimidate and threaten them; and attack, shock and stun them." Shamsher Khan replied forcefully.

"Is Kashmir going to become an independent sovereign nation, if we do that?" Abdul Aziz asked.

"Undoubtedly, Yes!" Shamsher Khan replied instantly.

"Shamsher *Bhai;* Killings, persecution and harassment of innocent persons are inhumane acts and un-Islamic too. If we indulge in savage and barbaric acts against innocents, we shall be defamed internationally, and, I am afraid, the 'Independence movement' of Kashmiris will fall flat. I beg to differ with you." Abdul Aziz replied.

Shamsher Khan did not react, and instead, he panned his steady looks at the face of Mohammad Anwar to evoke his reaction. Mohammad Anwar promptly said to Abdul Aziz, "Aziz *Bhai*, you are talking against purpose, target and aim, please be rationale".

"Do you think that Kashmiri Muslims lack intelligence, compassion and sensitivity? Do you believe that Kashmiri are going to act like savages? If you think so, you are mistaken, my friend." Mohammad Anwar said, staring into the eyes of Abdul Aziz.

Mohammad Anwar's words angered Abdul Aziz, and noisy arguments ensued between the two, which led to a scuffle.

Iqbal Cheema separated the two from coming to blows; and asked Abdul Aziz to cool down. In reply, angry Abdul Aziz told Iqbal Cheema that he should ask Mohammad Anwar to mend his supercilious attitude, and not him.

Shamsher Khan and Iqbal Cheema were caught off guard while witnessing the open conflict of opposing ideologies between the two. Haji Yusuf Dar handled the situation skillfully, and made both Mohammad Anwar and Abdul Aziz hug each other. At his instance, a traditional Kashmiri refreshment including mutton cutlets were served to the guests and the situation returned to normal; and Abdul Aziz resumed the conversation.

Abdul Aziz said to Shamsher Khan, "I am sorry, sir! I was blunt in expressing my opinion. Please tell me if we hound-out non-Muslims from the valley, is that going to give teeth to our struggle for 'Azadi'?

"Yes, Aziz B*hai,* I shall explain to you! The exodus of Hindus shall give birth to a scenario of confusion and disorder in the valley; local police and Indian security forces deployed in the valley shall get discredited; the political establishment of India shall get unnerved; the local administration shall overreact by asking the security forces to handle the situation with a heavy hand; and the security forces will go berserk. The infringement of civil liberties and use of brute force by the security forces shall create unrest in masses, and an alarming upsurge in human rights violations shall be inevitable. Human rights groups, world over, shall raise their voices, and that will give India a bad name. The situation will be quite conducive for Pakistan to serve a blow to India. With the support of a large number of Armed *Mujahedeen*, Pakistan's regular army shall lock horns with the Indian Army and security forces at multiple locations. With the grace and mercy of *Allah*, Pakistan Army shall create a new history by seceding Kashmir from India; and avenge Pakistan's disintegration of 1971."

Abdul Aziz's body language and facial expressions suggested that he was not prepared to buy the hypothesis of Shamsher Khan. He roared with long laughter and said, "Shamsher Khan *Bhai*, I am amused to hear your words; and it sounds like Bram Stoker's vampire fiction tale, *Dracula.* Pakistan may have scripted this action plan to avenge the humiliating defeat of 1971 war with India, but I don't see anything of that kind happening in Kashmir."

Major Shamsher Khan and Subedar Iqbal Cheema, in-service Army personnel of Pakistan, employed their motivating skills and every persuasive argument in their armory to win over Abdul Aziz for making him act like a tamed house-cat, but could not achieve what they wanted. Dissenting from the opinion of Shamsher Khan, Abdul Aziz could not hide his anger, and he left unceremoniously.

Although Abdul Aziz's unexpected reactions and unceremonious withdrawal surprised Shamsher Khan and Iqbal Cheema, yet they were not disappointed. They asked Haji Yusuf Dar and Mohammad Anwar to persuade Abdul Aziz. "Haji sahib, Abdul Aziz is a racing cyclist, we need to stop him from going to high-tech racing features." Shamsher Khan said to Haji Yusuf Dar while handing over an envelope, containing Rupees one lakh in Indian currency, for delivering to him.

After receiving a telephonic call from the Guest House that sleuths from the Foreigners Registration Office, Srinagar, had visited the guest house to contact the guests, Haji Yusuf Dar whispered into the year of Shamsher Khan, and the latter along with Iqbal Cheema cut short their visit in Srinagar city, and left for some unknown destination in a cab.

> *"Society and family as its psycho social agent, has to solve a difficult problem: How to break a person's will without his being aware of it? Yet by complicated process of indoctrination, rewards, punishments, and fitting ideology, it solves this task by and large so well that most people believe they are following their*

own will and are unaware that their will itself is conditioned and manipulated."

– Erich Fromm

3

Coerced Exodus, For Achieving Homogeneity

Spring had arrived in the beautiful valley of Kashmir in the year 1990; and nature was in her finest moods. With the melting of snow, the pansies, narcissi and daises had appeared on the mountain landscapes; and the almonds, apricots and cherries were shooting out of buds under the blue skies, bright sunshine and fresh air.

Life had reappeared in new colors with flowering of blossoms everywhere in Kashmir after the harsh winter months, and the natives of the land were rejoicing the arrival of spring. For the miniscule minority community members, aborigines of the valley, the story was quite different. They had been coerced to leave the land of their ancestors, and were wandering in their own country in search of emergency shelters and essentials for survival; they were scattered across the length and breadth of the country; and their faces presented the gloomy expressions of appalled hearts and faint spirits wherever they were.

After the exodus of minority Hindus of Kashmir from their homeland, which started in January 1990, Niranjan Nath, persuaded by one of his majority community neighbors, had stayed back with his family in his ancestral village in south Kashmir.

On the eve of *Navreh*, the New Year Day, which Kashmiri Pandits celebrate in the month of *chaitra* of V*ikram era,* on first day of bright fortnight, Niranjan Nath and his wife Dulari started the ritual of "*Thaal-Barun*"– neatly arranging walnuts, fresh flowers, Acorus calamus, a herb called '*Wye'* in Kashmiri, New Year almanac etc over a mound of rice in a large bronze plate called *Thaal.* After finishing the task of *Thaal-Barun*, Niranjan Nath asked his wife, Dulari, to keep the *Thaal*, the bronze pot, on a table in the living room for first-seeing in *Brahm-mohrat,* the wee hours, of New Year's Day.

Kaaboom! A deafening sound echoed Dulari's ears immediately after she lifted the bronze pot in her hands; and she felt the earth suddenly trembling. Frightened by the loud thud and sudden trembling of earth, she dropped the *Thaal;* and the rice grains, flowers, and other items got scattered over the floor. The unexplained boom with no visible sign of its cause made Niranjan Nath dumbfounded for a while; and he started reciting the *mantra 'Om Namah Shivai'*. He lifted the *Sapt-rishi* era almanac from the floor in his hands, stared at Lord *Krishna's* picture on its cover page; closed his eyes to soak his mind into a state of meditation; and started practising *Pranayama,* the practice of breath regulation. His wife collected the scattered grains of rice and other items of the *Thaal,* and arranged those afresh. Initially, Niranjan Nath had guessed that the large thud and fierce vibrations were due to some seismic activity, but subsequently he thought to himself that it could have been due to an IED blast caused by the terrorists.

While Niranjan Nath was introspecting and just settling in for the night, the battery-operated ticking-wall-clock in the living room struck 10. The abrupt barking of a dog in the unfenced courtyard of his house followed by the sound of knocking on the entrance door at odd hours startled him; he swiftly looked through the peep-hole; and opened the door for Mohi-ud-din, his neighbor.

At the entrance door, Mohi-ud-din, looking frightened and dejected, said to Niranjan Nath in a choked voice, "Alas! Oh *Nera,* these senseless zealots are hell-bent on converting our peaceful valley into a vast graveyard."

"What happened, *Mehda*?" Niranjan Nath asked.

"Just now, the senseless people caused a bomb explosion in the school building, and reduced it to rubble." Worrying Mohi-ud-din said.

Niranjan Nath held the hand of exasperated Mohi-ud-din, and conducted him to the living room of his home.

Mohi-ud-Din was a neighbor of Niranjan Nath, and both knew each other deeply. Niranjan Nath was a retired Headmaster of the school education department, and Mohi-ud-Din was an empanelled contractor of the state public works department. Close friends and neighbors, as they were, both called each other by short names – *Mehda* and *Nera*. Mohi-ud-Din was nick named as *Mehda Khoftan* too. He had remained a member of 'Peace-brigade' during Ghulam Mohammad Bakhshi's regime in Kashmir for some time; and the suffix '*Khoftan*' to his short name had been coined by Bakhshi's political opponents to ridicule the peace-brigade members. In Kashmir, Mohi-ud-Din and Niranjan Nath are called by short names *Mehda* and *Nera* respectively even today.

For quite some time, Niranjan Nath had been burning with curiosity about genesis and the growth of terror in Kashmir. He wanted to have a discourse with a person of sound judgment and common sense, and for that, Mohi-ud-Din's visit to his home at late hours was a God-sent opportunity. Initiating the discourse, Niranjan Nath said to Mohi-ud-Din, "*Mehda*, I want to know how and why 'terror' engulfed the peaceful valley of Kashmir?" Mohi-ud-Din chuckled to himself, and the response to Niranjan Nath's question was met with an awkward silence. Both looked at each other with a meaningful smile, and Niranjan Nath posed yet another direct question to Mohi-ud-Din: "*Mehda,* Did you go to the site of explosion?"

"Yes, I am coming from there only." Mohi-ud-Din replied.

"Why do they indulge in destruction of public property and abhorrent acts of violence?" Niranjan Nath asked.

"Because they do not know what they are doing."Down hearted Mohi-ud-Din said.

"What do you mean by saying that 'they do not know what they do', I can't understand that." Niranjan Nath asked with a sweet smile.

"*Nera,* you must be aware of the fact that at the time of the division of the Indian subcontinent on religious lines in 1947, a section of the majority population of Kashmir, driven by the ideology of theocracy, wanted to become part of the Islamic Republic of Pakistan; and another section of Kashmiri Muslims, driven by the ideology of having their own government, wanted J&K to become a nation-state." Mohi-ud-Din replied instantly.

"Yes, I know that, but why do you choose to reply my question by posing me a question? I am curious to know many things, and I want you to answer my simple question in a straight-forward manner." Niranjan Nath said with a smile.

"*Nera*, according to my understanding of the situation and developments, Pakistan has succeeded in forging a relationship between the two varying ideologies for achieving the object of seceding Kashmir from India." Mohi-ud-Din replied instantly.

"Now, what I see is that the forces of mayhem have engaged themselves in causing death and destruction in Kashmir valley. Are they going to achieve the goal of seceding J&K from India?" Niranjan Nath asked.

"*Nera*, they are mere puppets, working on the instructions of their mentors." Mohi-ud-Din said, shaking his head in disgust.

"Who instructs and supports them?" Niranjan Nath asked.

"*Nera*, it is none other than our neighboring country. Pakistan is surreptitiously supporting and providing logistic support to its cultivated agents in the valley." Mohi-ud-Din said.

"*Mehda*, tell me how?" Niranjan Nath asked.

"Don't ask me stupid questions, *Nera,* don't you know that Pakistan has been regularly pumping money, weapons and explosives to its saboteur agents through the line of control, using the services of guides and couriers. Don't you know that the weapons of destruction are not grown by peasants in paddy, maize or saffron fields of Kashmir?" Irritated Mohi-ud-Din said, shaking his head in disgust.

"Do you mean to say that Pakistan is directly involved in this dirty game?" Niranjan Nath asked, inquisitively.

"Yes, Pakistan has been meddling in the affairs of Kashmir for long. It has been using every trick in the book to divide Kashmir civil society; It spares no effort to whip up emotions of the majority population of the state by spreading malicious falsehood and fake narratives; and it wants to generate a feeling of discontent among the Muslims of J&K for creating hatred and mistrust against India. This is not for no reason- Pakistan wants to undermine Indian government's hold over the territory of J&K, preparatory to achieving its political objective. Equipping the saboteur-agents with weapons and explosives, and activating them to cause death and destruction in Kashmir, is aimed at creating chaos, disorder and panic." Mohi-ud-Din replied in a detestable tone.

"What is the political objective of Pakistan?" Niranjan Nath asked.

"Pakistan has a determined desire to extend its territories by annexing Kashmir with it, by hook or by crook." Mohi-ud-Din said.

"Do you think that Pakistan can achieve that?" Niranjan Nath asked.

"No, I don't think, but I have no reservation in accepting the fact that Pakistan has achieved much desired success in preparing the ground by radicalizing a cross-section of the majority population in Kashmir to the hilt." Mohi-ud-Din replied with expressions of disappointment.

"M*ehda*; if Pakistan wants to annex Kashmir with it, how come it supports the so called 'Independence movement of Kashmir'?" Niranjan Nath asked.

"O' *Nera*, I think, you have dispatched your intellect to the pasture, where the cattle graze green grass. There is always something more than what meets your eye. The irrational rhetoric of '*Azadi*' is nothing but a camouflage to blur the vision of reality; and this is hypocrisy, aimed at hoodwinking the international community." Mohi-ud-Din replied.

"Do you think that Pakistan shall succeed in its nefarious design?" Niranjan Nath asked.

"Whether or not it succeeds, I don't know, but it has consolidated its strength by luring hundreds of gullible youth. *Nera*, you will be surprised to know that the muddy water has flooded my home too!" Mohi-ud-Din said, with a long sigh.

"What do you mean to say?" Niranjan Nath asked.

"Yes, my friend, *Nera*. They have lured my younger son too." Sobbing Mohi-ud-Din replied.

"Oh my God, that is shocking! For me, it is hard to swallow that Nazir has subscribed to their ideology. How long this turbulence will last?" Shocked Niranjan Nath asked.

"I foresee that virtue is not going to subsist in Kashmir valley in a short time from now because hundreds of uncultivated minds have assented to the scheme of mad people." Sobbing Mohi-ud-Din said.

"*Mehda*, what is going to happen?" Niranjan Nath asked.

"*Nera,* neither Pakistan is going to succeed in its nefarious designs to secede Kashmir from India nor is anything soothing and productive going to happen for the natives of Kashmir." Mohi-ud-Din said in an easy-going tone.

"Don't you expect the situation in Kashmir to turn out well soon?" Niranjan Nath asked.

"*Nera*, Kashmir is in flames; peace-loving people are becoming the targets of gun wielding agents of the enemy country; the so-called mainstream politicians of Kashmir appear to have pledged their support to the forces of mayhem stealthily; and the Indian state is watching the situation helplessly which is quite appalling. Although I always see the positive side of things yet I find peace in the valley drifting apart." Mohi-ud-Din said, with teary eyes.

The wall-clock stroked 12. Mohi-ud-Din left hurriedly, and Niranjan Nath and Dulari saw him off at the outer gate of their house.

In the bed-room, Niranjan Nath breathed out a sigh of disgust, and said to his wife, "Dulari, I can't understand why negative feelings of fear have gripped me. You have always been telling me that I have a strong power of intuition."

"Undoubtedly, you have a strong power of intuition, I know that!" Dulari replied with a smile.

"Dulari, my negative feelings are unceasingly knocking my intellect that something very unpleasant will happen. The situation is worsening day by day; and I think we must leave for a safe place as did the other members of our community." Niranjan Nath said.

"Why do you think too hard of your gut-feelings? As long as Mohi-ud-Din *Bhai-Jan* is with us, we need not to worry." Dulari replied.

"Dulari, I am disturbed; Mohi-ud-Din too is not safe, and I have the apprehension that something bad is going to befall us. For the first time in my life today, I saw the *Navreh Thaal* falling from your hands; and that is not a good omen." Niranjan Nath said.

Dulari stared at her husband and said, "Don't you lean too much on your instincts, take it easy."

Mohi-ud-Din was intercepted at gunpoint by three masked men and whisked away to some unknown destination, immediately after he left Niranjan Nath's home. Despite hearing his loud arguments with the abductors, his neighbors did not dare to come out of their houses, out of fear; and one of the abductors shouted aloud that he was being taken for lip-sewing to shut his mouth.

Niranjan Nath and his wife had not even the faintest inkling of the ghastly incident until 6:00 am of the *Navreh*-day. Rumors were going around the village and adjoining areas that Mohi-ud-Din was mercilessly beaten to death by three gun-wielding *Mujahedeen.*

Niranjan Nath and his wife Dulari rushed to Mohi-ud-Din's residence. A persistent pall of hopelessness and helplessness had overtaken the family members of Mohi-ud-Din. Mohi-ud-Din's elder son, Hassan, confided to Niranjan Nath that a Kashmiri speaking young man, wearing black color monkey-cap with two small openings for eyes, holstering a pistol to his waist belt, had come to their residence at around 5:00 am: and informed them that no physical harm was caused to Mohi-ud-Din after his abduction, and if we wanted to see him alive,

Mohi-ud-Din's younger son, Nazir, must surrender before the area commander within 12 hours.

Replying to probing questions by Niranjan Nath, Hassan said, "Uncle, a week before, at around 9:00 pm, the same person had come to our home and asked my father to meet Tiger Khan, Area Commander, in a nearby orchard for an urgent talk; and he warned my father to be prepared for severe punishment if he failed to show up within half an hour."

"Who is Tiger Khan, Area Commander, and what had he to talk to Mohi-ud-din?" Niranjan Nath asked.

"Uncle, Shakir Khan is a Punjabi speaking mercenary from Pakistan. He is code named as 'Tiger Khan', and is the Area Commander of a group of terrorists in our area. I don't know what he had to say, but I guess that he wanted to dissuade my father from showing dissent to his diktats". Hassan said, with tearful eyes.

Yes, I can understand, he must have been told that Mohi-ud-din shall not subscribe to the acts of a savage person." Niranjan Nath said.

"Uncle, I am worried; my father shall never give assent to his diktats; and he will never deviate from the righteous path." Sobbing Hassan said, with tears running down his face.

"Did you ask your brother, Nazir, to meet Tiger Khan?" Niranjan Nath asked.

"Uncle, I have not seen him for the last 3-4 days. What I know is that my brother was a member of Tiger Khan's outfit, but he deserted him. He has become a member of some other faction; and his whereabouts are not known to me". Hassan replied.

Niranjan Nath and Hassan were busy devising a strategy to get Mohi-ud-din released unharmed, and they received a shocking information that Nazir was spotted hanging by a rope from a walnut tree in the adjoining village; and the police had reached the spot. Unable to comprehend what had happened, stunned Hassan and Niranjan Nath left for the spot and saw the dead body of Nazir, already taken into possession by the Police for postmortem.

A handwritten note had been recovered by the police from the pocket of Nazir; and the content of the note revealed that Nazir was forced to take up the gun under compelling circumstances, only to protect his family from the wrath of Tiger Khan. The note further stated that Nazir's father had been held captive to pressurize him to surrender, what he was never going to do; and he had no other option available, but to end his own life to save the life of his innocent father. Hassan admitted the handwriting of the note was that of his brother.

Mohi-ud-din's elder son, Hassan, and Niranjan Nath waited to receive Nazir's dead body for final rites. To prevent an explosion of feelings and anger, they dispatched a family friend to Mohi-ud-din's residence to convey that the rumor of Nazir's suicide was a mere hoax, and negotiations with the abductors of Mohi-ud-din were in progress.

Mohi-ud-din was released, and he reached home at 9:00 pm. He had been physically tortured, and was in bad shape. The burn marks, caused by smoldering cigarettes all over his body, and bleeding lips, caused by pinning his lips with a paper stapler, revealed the beastly treatment meted out to him during the period of his captivity.

Mohi-ud-Din seemed unaware of the death of his son, and he revealed to his family members that during his captivity he could gather the information that Nazir had revolted against Tiger Khan by joining his rival faction; and bloodthirsty Tiger Khan was hell-bent on killing him. He further told his wife that Tiger Khan's gun-wielding men had spotted him near the site of an explosion, and later positioned themselves near the rear window of the living room of Niranjan Nath to hear the conversation between him and Niranjan Nath surreptitiously. He also confided to her that the gun wielding terrorists are bent on achieving homogeneity in Kashmir, by coercing the left over Kashmiri Pandits to leave their homeland; and according to Tiger Khan, the dreaded Pakistani mercenary, Niranjan Nath was a *Kafir*; and there was no space for infidels in Kashmir.

Mohi-ud-din wanted Niranjan Nath and his family to leave for a safe place as early as possible. He said to his wife, "Niranjan Nath has complete faith and trust in me, and till the day I die, I want to maintain the trust even at the cost of my life. For *Allah's* sake, tell him that he is facing imminent danger to his life." And, Mohi-Ud-Din's wife immediately conveyed the message to Dulari, wife of Niranjan Nath.

The dead body of Nazir, younger son of Mohi-Ud-Din, was handed over to Hassan for final rites by the police after observing legal formalities. Hassan and Niranjan Nath brought the dead body to Mohi-Ud-Din's residence at around 11pm. Upon seeing the dead body of his son, and after getting the detailed information from Hassan and Niranjan Nath regarding the circumstances that led to Nazir's death, Mohi-Ud-Din lost his mind. In a state of trauma and shock, he came running out of his house, and in a high pitched voice challenged Tiger khan to get ready to die a dog's death.

Nazir's dead body was placed in the house, and the wailing and weeping family members were waiting for the sun to rise to bury the dead body in his ancestral graveyard. Tiger Khan had issued a diktat to neighbors and relatives of the deceased to refrain from joining his funeral, and hand-written posters had been pasted at several conspicuous places in the area. The content of the hand-written posters read: "Nazir was a traitor; he was an enemy's agent, and an informer; and all those who shall attend his funeral ceremony shall be dispatched to hell."

Niranjan Nath had decided to say goodbye to his home and hearth, and he chose to seek leave from Mohi-ud-din and his family members. Immediately after midnight, he visited the residence of Mohi-ud-din, and said to Mohi-ud-din, "Mehda, the beautiful experiences of the past, you and I have shared together, reminisce my mind, but what the fate has decreed for us, we don't know. I am taking your leave, and to hand over the keys of my home. Please take care, and God willing, we shall meet again." Wailing and weeping Mohi-ud-Din gave Niranjan Nath a tight hug, and both wept bitterly.

Niranjan Nath's family, comprising his old mother, his wife, Dulari, and physically challenged son left the village in the dead of night, and the village got completely cleansed of Kashmiri Hindus, the aborigines of the land.

After the arrival of the full day light, Nazir's dead body was carried to the graveyard by his father, brother, uncle, and one of his cousins for the funeral ceremony. None of the neighbors or relatives of Mohi-ud-din dared to attend the funeral ceremony, because they had not the courage and boldness to dissent the diktat of Tiger Khan.

Hassan was shocked to see the staying away of his close friends and relatives from becoming a part of the funeral ceremony of his brother; and he solemnly pledged not to rest until he avenged the death of his innocent brother. He said to his father, "I want to protect my family members; I want to die fighting for the cause of humanity and restoration of peace in my homeland; and I want to fight against the beasts, bullies, rogues, and the villains of peace."

"But, how will you fight; they have automatic guns, and you are empty handed like a sitting duck? Mohi-ud-din asked.

"I shall equip myself with an automatic gun." Hassan said.

"Tell me, how?" Mohi-ud-din asked.

"I have decided to join the rival group of Tiger Khan, with the sole object of getting equipped with an automatic gun."

"I wish you success." Mohi-ud-din said with jubilation.

Hassan joined the rival faction of Tiger Khan, the same day; and he became a member of a terrorist outfit.

Within a month of his taking up the gun, Hassan was killed in an internecine conflict between the two warring factions of terrorists operating in the area. Tiger Khan too was eliminated by the security forces within a few days of the killing of Hassan.

> *"It's like that old story-you can't keep your snakes in your backyard and expect them to bite your neighbors. Eventually those snakes are going to turn on whoever has them in the backyard."*
>
> **– Ex American US Secretary of State's Message to Pakistan.**

4

Fragile Bulbuls, And the Hawks

Gash Lal belonged to a remote village in North Kashmir. Born in an affluent Kashmiri Brahmin family, he was well versed in Sanskrit literature and Persian poetry, and had a thorough grasp of philosophical verses of Lallishvari *yogini,* the *Shruks* of *Sufi* saint Noor-ud-din Noorani and teachings of a host of *Sufis* and Saints of Kashmir. For his humanistic and social behavior, he was held in high esteem by Muslims and Hindus, both. Courageous and fearless, as he was, Gash Lal chose not to leave his ancestral village at the time of the en masse exodus of Hindus from the valley; and he stayed back in his ancestral village.

It was May-Day of 1990, the International Worker's Day. The snow had begun to melt on the higher-reaches of the valley of Kashmir; the sunshine, descending on the mountain tops had caused the glaciers to melt; waterfalls were in sight on mountain slopes; and the dry brooks including the one adjacent to Gash Lal's residential house had rejuvenated. Gash Lal's family, comprising his son, Ashok, daughter in law, Shyama, and grandson, Ajeet, was the lone Hindu family living in the village of their ancestors.

The daylight had already faded, and it was fully dark. A gentle cold breeze blowing in the ancestral village of Gash Lal was delightful. The harmony of the gushing water of the rejuvenated brook, adjacent to his house, had made his family members feel ecstatic, but it was not so for Gash Lal. He appeared lost in thoughts, and quite disenthralled by the beauty of nature. His son, Ashok, had noticed him taking deep sighs intermittently since morning; and had comprehended that the unusual long sighs of his father were the manifestation of an unknown worry brewing up in his mind.

Around 9 pm, after finishing dinner, Gash Lal, as usual, sat down on a '*Takhtposh*', a table-like wooden platform, for *Huqaa*-smoking; Ashok filled the funnel-shaped earthen '*Chillum*' of Hubble-bubble with tobacco and light charcoal, and ignited a fire in '*Chillum*'. Before sucking the typical wooden pipe, called *'Nai',* the indigenous Kashmiri wooden pipe, to draw the smoke of tobacco into his mouth, Gash Lal again had a deep sigh, and simultaneously, he hit his forehead with hand. Ashok asked his father instantly, "Dear dad, you appear tense and worried, why?"

"Over the years, I had been observing that the religious zealots and fundamentalists in Kashmir were busy inflaming and provoking the peace-loving and credulous Kashmiri Muslims for xenophobic reactions; and, for quite some time, I have been helplessly watching, right in front of my eyes, the astute manipulations of fanatics, working in pursuit of their religious ideals, poisoning the minds of Kashmiri Muslims to discompose the serene life in my homeland. During Fri-day mass prayers of the majority community, I had been regularly hearing the religious speeches of the non-Kashmiri preachers, from the public address system of a nearby mosque, for many years. Besides delivering sermons for strictly observing the adherence of Islamic teachings, the *Deobandi* preachers, through their oratory skills, used to stimulate the emotions of the people in attendance against the infidels and idolaters." Gash Lal replied instantly.

"That has happened in the past, but why are you tensed up now, dear dad?"" Ashok asked hurriedly.

"My dear son, although I smelt a rat yet I did not throw up my hands in despair and helplessness, and vowed to live in the valley, and resisted leaving even when the members of the minuscule minority were being selectively targeted. I confess that I have erred in my judgment for the first time in my life by not looking at the wider aspect of the emerging situation in my homeland." Gash Lal replied emphatically.

"Dear dad, please tell me why are you tensed up now?" Ashok asked curiously.

"Ashok, you know well that I don't get scared easily, but that does not mean I enjoy watching dreaded real-life horror!" Gash Lal said with grossed out face.

"Dear dad, I could not comprehend your symbolic and abstract reply, please elaborate." Ashok asked.

"Listen, dear son; this morning, I trembled when a Muslim friend informed me that you and I, both, have been branded as 'infidels' and 'informers', the 'enemies of Islam', by a terrorist outfit; and a diktat has been issued to the villagers to boycott us socially. I may be wrong, but I believe that after the search operation conducted by the security forces two days ago, which led to the recovery of weapons and explosives from a house in our village, our friends and neighbors have perhaps started suspecting us as–informers of the security forces." Gash Lal said with a heavy heart.

Although Ashok too had grasped well the paradigm of the changing social dynamics in the valley, yet he wanted to know the reaction of his father. He said to his father, "Don't you think that majority of Kashmiri Muslims are peace-loving, and they, in no circumstance, shall get carried away or excited by any seduction or allurement?"

"Show me a single most courageous and brave soul of our village, not fearing the gun, shadow of death and irretrievably risky position? I have been seeing that the voice of the peace-loving Muslims of the valley is being silenced by the gun-wielding freebooters." Gash Lal said with expressions of repugnance looming large on his face.

"Why?" Ashok said.

"My most trusted Muslim friends and neighbors have confided to me that a band of freebooters has been pushed into the valley of Kashmir by Pakistan to carry out serial bomb explosions and random firings for causing ghastly deaths to scare the people of the valley in general and minority Hindus in particular." Gash Lal replied grimly.

"Dad, they are gun-wielding mercenaries. Why do you call them freebooters?" Ashok asked.

"They are human beings just like you and me, but without any regard for human values, acceptable behavior and standard principles of human dignity, and they carry out all sorts of despicable acts at the behest of their mentors unhesitatingly." Gwash Lal said.

Ashok intentionally looked towards the entry door of the lobby, to avoid a direct eye contact with his father, and said, "Dear dad, I think we should not be too worried because our Muslim friends and neighbors shall guard us against any hostile attitude or improper behavior of these freebooters."

"I wish my apprehensions are proved wrong, but wishes are mere desires, not the reality." Gash Lal said, shaking his head.

Gash Lal's mind was deeply rooted in the inheritance of the centuries-old legacy of 'tolerance', 'co-existence' and 'brotherhood' of his homeland. He was dismayed to see that the secessionist groups and over-ground mainstream political actors, covertly backed by Pakistan, were engaged in besieging the centuries-old *Kashmiriyat.* He had grasped it well, belatedly though, that a section of youth, numerically small though, had been indoctrinated by Pakistan's stooges to create discord between various sections of the civil society of Kashmir, and they were trained in guerrilla-warfare and handling and using of modern and sophisticated weapons in various training camps of Pakistan.

Gash Lal confided to his son all that had been grasped by him about the Kashmir imbroglio. The interaction between the father-son continued for about two hours; and before going to sleep, Gash Lal started his routine session of transcendental meditation.

It was around 11 pm, and the untoward happened–Gash Lal's house was pelted with stones in the dead of night by unknown people, and the showering of stones on CGI-roof of his house, one after another, made loud thuds!

Terrified Gash Lal sprang from the wooden platform to peep through the cavity of a window. He was surprised to find two street lamps, installed on nearby electric poles, turned off, and the entire area engulfed in darkness. Intermittent stone-pelting on his CGI-roofed house, causing large thuds, continued for more than 15 minutes without any respite, but no one living in his immediate neighborhood came out to see what had happened; and that set Gash Lal's teeth on edge.

A bead of sweat on the forehead of Gash Lal and his breathlessness clearly indicated that he was terrified; and he hurriedly lay on the bed-like wooden platform. He started gasping, and told Ashok in a hoarse voice, "Ashok, the process of manifestation and dissolution has been in place from times immemorial. I was born in the land of my ancestors, the land of great saints and seers, and I shall be lucky enough if I die here."

Gash Lal's words triggered whimpering and emotional tears in Ashok, Shyama and Ajeet.

Gash Lal complained of discomfort, chest and back pain with shortness of breath; and started reciting *'Om Namah Shivay'* mantra. Ashok observed that he was breathing laboriously, and gasping for air. He started giving him mentholated ointment chest-rub, and Shyama and Ajeet started massaging his feet with mustard oil. Gash Lal looked at the face of his son directly, and said in a weak voice, "Ashok, I think our Muslim friends and neighbors have accepted the diktats of the forces of mayhem because of the fear of gun." Ashok nodded his head in approval.

Gash Lal's condition was fast deteriorating; his breathing was interrupted by gasping; his breaths were irregular; and his eyes were not blinking normally. He was a conscious person on the verge of dying; and he screamed incoherently, "Ashok, it is not safe for you to live here now; and I want you to forfeit your home and leave with Shyama and little Ajeet early morning to some safe place, but promise me that, after I die, you shall consign my body to fire in my ancestral cremation ground, near the orchard, and immerse the ashes at the confluence of '*Vitasta*' and '*Sindhu*' at Shadipora and '*prayag*' at Allahabad." Ashok comforted him by holding his right hand in his own hands; and promised to fulfill his dying wish. Within a few minutes, Gash Lal suffered a massive heart attack; and breathed his last.

Destiny had willed to fulfill the last wish of Gash Lal, a 67-year old Kashmiri Hindu. He had a frail body, though mentally agile and physically fit; and his son, Ashok, and daughter in law, Shyama, had no difficulty in carrying the dead body to the cremation ground on a homemade stretcher. A pile of firewood had been stacked by Gash Lal for drying in his orchard, adjacent to the cremation ground, about a month ago. The same firewood was used to consign his body to flames.

Ashok was in a hurry to collect the ashes for immersion at Shadipora and Prayag to fulfill the last wish of his father. He, along with his wife and son, waited in vain at the cremation ground, till twilight, for the smolders and burning charcoal to extinguish and the ashes to cool; and finally he sprinkled water to stop flameless burning charcoal. The wet ashes were filled in two earthenware urns, and the trio left for their home.

It was the time of Isha-prayer for Muslims in Kashmir valley, the time of offering *Namaz,* the time to remember God's presence, guidance, mercy and forgiveness before retiring for the night; and Gash Lal's son Ashok, his wife, Shyama, and son, Ajeet, carrying two earthenware pots, were returning home, tired and totally exhausted.

The high pitched noise of stone-pelting of preceding night continually echoed in Ashok's ears; his eyes had turned red and puffy because of the sleepless night and physical exertion for the whole day; and his wife Shyama and young Ajeet were in shock, totally exhausted and yawning continuously.

Ashok and his wife placed the two urn pots on the ground; and while pushing the entry door of his home, Ashok found a handwritten poster adhering to the wall. "*Mukhbir Ashok Batta,* leave the village by tomorrow morning ; treat this warning seriously; and don't force us to issue *fatwa* for dispatching you to hell." was the content of the poster, written in the Urdu language. It took Ashok some time to read the 3-line content of the poster, but the content of the poster made him just down in the dumps almost instantly. Frightened and dejected Ashok, along with his wife and son, walked into a room, and placed the earthenware urns on a shelf.

In a few minutes, a gentle knock sounded from the back-door of Ashok's house, and Shyama said, "Who is there?"

The person knocking at the door said, "I am Rashid Khan, Shyama *Bhabi.*"

Shyama opened the door; and Rashid plunged in hurriedly and bolted the door from inside. Looking completely worried and disturbed, Rashid Khan mumbled, "My dearest friend, Ashok; I can't stay here for more than a minute because the gun-wielding people, which include my own close acquaintances too, are monitoring every movement and activity in the village. I don't want anything bad befalling you and your family; and you need to leave the village for some safe place as early as possible. Ashok, please don't walk up to the cab boarding-point by road, and instead walk through the paddy fields; Mustaffa and I shall be observing you secretly; and you need not worry."

Trembling with fear, Ashok said, "My dear friend, we are tired and completely exhausted; and we shall have to cover a long distance on foot to catch a cab for the onward journey. What shall we do?"

With tears trickling down his cheeks, Rashid Khan looked completely numbed out for about a minute after seeing Ashok, Shyama and Ajeet sighing and crying. He clasped Ashok tightly in his arms, and said, "Ashok, you know that the social and moral bedrock in the valley has rotted; and, for the last few years, it has taken a back seat to fundamentalism and religious intolerance. They suspect you as an informer of security forces; and they can go to any extent– Please, for my sake, don't compromise on the safety of your life; and don't you become a sitting duck. I strongly advise you to leave for a safe place as early as possible, and I shall ensure that the cab driver shall wait for you outside his home to pick you up."

Rashid Khan and Ashok were neighbors and bosom friends; he wanted to be with Ashok for more time to share his grief, despair and pain, but he could not tame his fears. He gave him rupees ten thousand for meeting the travelling expenses, and Ashok accepted the money without any reservation. With tears streaming down his face, Ashok hugged Rashid Khan, and asked him to harvest the crops of cherries from his orchard if he did not return soon, and to keep the sale proceeds with him. With tears rolling down his cheeks, Rashid Khan again hugged Ashok, and left after a tender gaze on his face.

During the day, Ashok had made up his mind to leave for some safe destination with his wife and little son, but his tired mind was incapacitated to decide on the manner of leaving. Mentally upset, physically exhausted and yawning continuously, Ashok said to his wife, "Shyama, I don't know what to do?"

"We must leave this place as early as possible." Shyama replied instantly.

"Shyama, I am completely broken; the fear and exhaustion have made my senses numb; and I am just like a lazy pigeon, flying in the dark clouds of the sky, not far away from hawks."

Ashok and Shyama, both, cajoled their 12-year old Ajeet not to sleep and be prepared for the night journey. It was already dark, and Ashok and his wife decided to leave before the dawn at any cost. The trio had some bread and milk, and that provided them strength and vitality for sustaining physical and mental activity.

Ashok swiftly went to the cow-shed; set free the two jersey-breed cows and their two calves after applying vermilion-paste on their forehead to indicate that the cattle stood donated by the owner; locked the main entry-door of the house; and left for unknown destination with his wife and young Ajeet, only to join more than three hundred thousand Kashmiri Pandits, scattered across the country.

While walking through his vast ancestral orchards in the dark night, carrying the ashes of his father in two big earthenware urns, physically and mentally exhausted Ashok, in a state of self-absorption, started behaving abnormal–simultaneously murmuring and laughing in wild excitement, and conversing forcefully with some imaginary person, "How can fragile bulbuls fight with the falcons, and why should they hound singing bulbuls out of their nests?"

The harrowing experience of seeing the abnormal and imbecile behavior of her husband, Shyama took no time in grasping that her husband had sunk in maniac depression. Engulfed in a strong feeling of fear, Shyama felt that her body was becoming hollow and her mind disintegrating; and all of a sudden, she sat down under a walnut tree; and started shrieking. Ashok yelled at her, "What happened; why did you sit down like a lame lamb; you want me to get killed?"

After a brief halt of a few minutes, they restarted their journey, and walked a distance of nearly 7 miles up to the main road and boarded a cab for the unknown destination!

Ashok waited and waited for more than three decades for the sun to rise and shine in the land of his ancestors with the fond hope of the arrival of spring after the melting of frozen snow, but that did not happen. He lived the life of a refugee in his own country till he breathed his last in 2020!

> *"The creation of India and Pakistan were pyrrhic victories for their denizens because the political, socioeconomic, psychological and cultural havoc wreaked by that momentous event is reflected in those pogroms, ethnic cleansing, proliferation of nuclear weapons, poverty and riots that continue to cause seismic tremors in the Indian subcontinent."*
>
> **– Nyla Ali Khan**

5

Abhimanyu in 'Chakravyuh'

On May 1, 1990, the International Workers-Day, daylight had faded; birds had returned to their night-time roosting locations after flying and foraging the whole day; and the night-owls were becoming active. Jai Koul tilted his head skywards, and gazed at the full blazing stars through the window of the first floor of his house; and then closed his eyes for a while to design a plan for the fifth birthday celebrations of his son, Abhimanyu. Abruptly, a muzzle flash of the gun reached his eyes, and the deafening sound of the burst-firing hit his ears. Since the terrorists had been active in the valley for quite some time, Jai Koul could comprehend in no time that it was an act of terror perpetrated by the terrorists. Jai Koul hurriedly walked up to the entry gate of his house to check what exactly had happened, and Abimanyu followed him.

Jai Koul was thunderstruck to see his brother, Pitambar, lying in a pool of blood; having been hit with multiple rounds of fire, his head was severed into pieces; and his life had come to an end. A large size Teddy-bear gift, a packet of balloons and a chocolate box were scattered pell-mell over the ground near the dead body, and a cardboard tag, attached with the teddy-bear gift carried the personalized wish for Abhimanyu, artistically written and signed by Pitambar. The 5-year old

Abimanyu became a witness to the most ghastly tragedy of terror, the gruesome murder of his uncle.

Jai Koul belonged to a village in the vicinity of saffron town of Pampore in the Kashmir valley, and was a renowned commission and forwarding agent of Kashmiri saffron. In Kashmiri language 'Kong-*Posh'* denotes 'saffron flower'; Jai Koul was popularly known as *'Kong-Posh'*, a name given to him by the trader fraternity of saffron in the valley. In addition to a large area of Saffron-land, acquired through inheritance, he owned a 3-story modern house with all the tangible assets for comfortable lifestyle in a middle-class household. Pitambar was the younger brother of Jai Koul. His wife Bimla was a teacher, working in a public school; and Pitambar, a bachelor, was an employee of a private insurance company.

The body of Pitambar was cremated on May 2. After returning from the cremation ground, panic stricken Jai Koul had not even a spark of hope that the situation in Kashmir was going to improve in the near future. He wanted to shift his family to a safe place urgently. It was hard for him and his family members to bid adieu to moderate climate of their homeland, snow-clad mountains, lush green meadows with serene surroundings, graceful lakes and wetlands, mighty Chinars, and the land of a large variety of temperate fruits and saffron etc, but for saving their lives, they had no other option.

Despairing Jai Koul, along with his family members, started his journey in the large compartment of a goods vehicle before the arrival of dawn on May 3. The family members were besieged by the thoughts of awful experiences, they had to live through, away from home. The fear that gun-wielding terrorists would show no mercy in targeting them was continually lurking at the back of their minds; and their faces were gloomy. Deep down, Jai Koul knew that he was moving to settle in a humid subtropical climate, and to start life afresh in a new social, cultural and economic setup, which was not going to be an easy task.

The bright sun was about to hide in the black despair of night, and the helpless and hapless Jai Koul's family reached Jammu, the city of temples. It was most fatiguing, stressful and a nap-less day for little Abhimanyu; and throughout the day, he made repeated enquiries from his mother, and father about Pitambar and the teddy-bear gift.

Fondly called 'Abhay' by his family members, Abhimanyu was admitted to a Play-way school when he was just 3-year old. He was an example of acceptable behavior, both at school and at home. He was in the process of exploring the world, and developing the ability to feed his mind with new experiences of life, but after witnessing the dead body of his uncle lying in a pool of blood, he was badly shaken. He did not comprehend what had happened, but watching the wailing and weeping members of his family and the outburst of traumatic emotions of his father and mother, at the time of the funeral-march of his uncle, had impacted his psyche adversely.

Towards the beginning of 1990, gun wielding terrorists were visible in the valley of Kashmir, and the government was invisible. Terrorists had achieved much success in creating an atmosphere of confusion and chaos in the valley by demolishing the centuries-old unique cultural heritage, and the bondage of brotherhood. After the terrorists murdered many innocent minority community members in a killing spree across the length and breadth of the valley, hundreds of thousands of minority Hindus had left the valley to seek refuge in various parts of the country including the Jammu city, the winter capital of J&K state. The month of April, 1990 was the peak phase of the exodus of minuscule minority community from the valley of Kashmir.

Jai Koul's family reached the registration counter, set up by a social organization at Jammu. Catering to the heavy rush of Kashmiri Hindu community members, fleeing from the valley of Kashmir, was not an easy task; and the state administration had designated some school buildings as temporary shelter-homes for the internally displaced people. A small space, in one of the halls of a school building, was allotted to Jai Koul's family where six families had already been accommodated.

The shared accommodation provided to Jai Koul was neither sufficient nor appropriate, but he had no choice; and he along with his family members occupied the available space in one of the corners of the hall near the entry door.

Abhimanyu's regular sleeping schedule was disturbed and delayed for two consecutive nights. While the family members of Jai Koul were engaged in furnishing the space and arranging food etc, Abhimanyu watched everything curiously.

After eating, tired and exhausted, as he was, little Abimanyu fell asleep around 12 o'clock at midnight on a thin foam-mattress. Within a few minutes of sleep, he abruptly woke up; stared at the faces of all young and old in the crowded hall of the school building; and said to his mother, "Mom, we have so many uncles and aunties here, why don't they go to sleep in their bedrooms?" Within a few minutes, he quickly rolled over the floor-bed again and returned to sleep; and after some time, he woke up again and shrieked: "Mom, please switch off the lights and allow me to sleep."

Little Abhimanyu was highly irritated; and there were several variables combined together, which contributed to his irritation: He was feeling uncomfortable because the temperature in the valley was moderate at 17-18 degrees, and, after travelling a long distance in a load carrier, he had landed in Jammu city where the mercury had touched 36 degrees; he was used to sleeping in a comfortable bed-room environment, and overnight it had changed; and the bright lights, noise, and snoring of a stranger, an old lady, asleep next to him, disturbed his sleep.

After a while, Abhimanyu calmed down; moved his head from left to right, gazed at the environment and ambience of the surroundings in the hall; and said to his mother, "lousy; why no carpets? Shabby wall surfaces; why no paintings? Where are the beds to sleep on?" His mother held him close to her chest, and whispered into his ear," Abhay, look; everybody in the hall is deep asleep, you too must go to sleep now; and tomorrow we shall be back to our place." She started singing Kashmiri lullabies to aid his sleep.

Abimanyu had difficulty staying asleep because he was disturbed and emotionally upset, and his mind was not at rest. He got up swiftly and sat in the lap of his father, and said to him, "Why don't you get me my bed to sleep on?" Emotional arousals triggered tears of sadness in Jai Koul; and, in frustration, Abhimanyu's mother hit her forehead with her hand thrice.

After finding everybody asleep in the hall, little Abhimanyu fell asleep in the lap of his father for about two hours. He was awakened by the high pitch screaming of his mother, who was stung by some insect. Everyone in the hall was taken aback and they assembled near her floor-bed; and after Abhimanyu's grandmother lifted the bed-sheet, a black-color scorpion was found crawling on the mattress. Without knowing what had gone wrong, Abhimanyu also started screaming, but he again fell asleep after his mother was rushed to nearby hospital for first aid.

While his father and mother were away, little Abhimanyu repeatedly screamed after finding a centipede crawling near his pillow. His grandmother stomped on the centipede with footwear, and she soothed and comforted him to resettle. Frightened and confused, as he was, Abhimanyu started calling for his mother loudly, and the inmates of the temporary shelter home were all awakened.

Abhimanyu was completely disoriented. Meanwhile, his mother and father returned from the hospital, and out of blue, he said to his mother, "Mom, Pitambar uncle was in a deep sleep near the gate; he saw me approaching him, and stretched his hands to envelop me in his lap; he hugged me tightly, and gave me the teddy bear, chocolates and balloons; and I kissed him too." Abhimanyu's words charged the emotions of the grieving family members of his family, and they started wailing and weeping. The emotionally driven ladies and children of other families followed suit, and that again cast a gloom in the hall.

With each day Abhimanyu started showing impulsive and aggressive behavior; he became defiant, made an angry face every time, and indulged in naughty and nasty actions. The signs of psychosocial stress became visible in him. He often indulged in quarrelling with the children of other families living in the collective shelter home; disturbed them, and did not allow them to sleep; and often confined them in washrooms by bolting from outside, even at midnight. He not only disturbed the young, but the old too. Abhimanyu's disturbing behavior even angered a few insensitive inmates of the shelter home.

One day, while the inmates of the temporary shelter-camp, including his parents and grandmother, had queued-up in the school ground to collect edible items and other things from a social organization, Abhimanyu quietly engaged himself in cleaning the floor by sprinkling lumps of detergent and water and using his neighbor's turban as sponge. This virtually resulted in a scuffle between the two families. After a few days, in the morning, Abhimanyu was minutely observing an inmate of the shelter home trimming the unwanted hairs of his bushy and well-groomed moustache, extending up to his cheeks, with a pair of scissors; and while the person was having a short nap post-lunch, he took out the pair of scissors from his shaving-kit and trimmed the left side of his long moustache close to skin. The person woke up; and in a fit of anger kicked Abhimanyu in the face, which resulted in his bleeding from his nose. A scuffle ensued between the two families, and two counter cases came to be registered in the local police station; and the person was arrested. After the person was released on bail, he devised a noxious plan to teach little Abhimanyu and his parents a lesson.

While Abhimanyu was curiously watching the activities of mustachioed man from a distance, he took out hundreds of used safety razors from his shaving-kit box; after removing the blade guards of hundreds of used blades, he put the safety razors, in a haphazard pile, in the box; and left the hall. This was a trap laid for little Abhimanyu. He wasted no time in fiddling with the safety razors, and suffered multiple sharp-cut wounds in both hands. The floor got smeared with blood; and Abhimanyu suffered heavy blood loss. An altercation took place between the two families in the hall; and Abhimanyu was rushed to the hospital.

Jai Koul realized that Abhimanyu's mood, thinking and behavior were changing fast due to emotional disorder, and he needed immediate intervention from a psychotherapist. He had braved the most difficult situations with courage throughout his life. He had grasped the words of Lord Krishna that a man of wisdom, in no circumstance, must feel dejected, and must do his '*Karma*' till the end. The abnormal behavior and naughty actions of Abhimanyu haunted him continually, and he wanted to pull him out of the *Chakravyuh*, the circle of psychological disorder, in which he had been badly trapped.

Jai Koul decided to begin his life afresh, and work through the trauma of the death of his younger brother, and the loss of home and hearth and flourishing business, the debilitating effects of exodus. He exhibited the measure of his steady wisdom; and worked in the direction of alleviating the traumatic stress of little Abhimanyu.

Jai Koul contacted his friend, Haji Rasool, by phoning him. Haji Rasool, a native of Kashmir, was his bosom friend; and his friendship with Haji Rasool dated back to his college days. A decade ago, Haji Rasool had migrated to Khajoraho, MP, a place of top attraction for domestic and international tourists in

India, to establish a business of dry-fruit and handicrafts of Kashmir. Well connected with his roots, he used to pay frequent visits to Kashmir, and was quite familiar with all the family members of Jai Koul. Haji Rasool, a well-to-do person in Khajoraho, assured Jai Koul of every possible help, and invited him to come to Khajoraho along with family.

Jai Koul and his family travelled to Khajoraho by bus, and met Haji Rasool. Jai Koul's family was given a hearty and hospitable reception by Haji Rasool and his family. With his eyes flooded with tears, Jai Koul briefly narrated to Haji Rasool the heart-wrenching tale of woes, pain and persecution suffered by him, and he fainted twice. A pall of gloom hung over Haji Rasool and his family, and all of them were moved to tears. Haji Rasool tried to console Jai Koul, and said, "My dearest friend, I can understand what you are going through; I can never forget the help you have extended to me at a time when it was needed; and I swear to 'Allah' that I shall help you in every possible way to pull you out of the unfortunate and unpleasant situation. If I don't keep my word, I am a sinner; and you can rest assured."

The consoling words of Haji Rasool lit the candle of hope for Jai Koul, and he said nervously, "My friend, today I have discovered that not everything is lost; and in you I find the inherent fragrance of my heritage and composite ethos."

"My friend, don't you ever give up hope for a brighter tomorrow. It is only a fraction of the population of Kashmir and a small section of insurgents who wreaked havoc in our peaceful homeland, not all. Kashmir society is pious theosophical; and the dust and dirt in our homeland shall get cleaned definitely, it may take some time." Haji Rasool said.

Haji Rasool made little Abhimanyu sit in his lap, and said to him, "Within two or three days, I shall decorate a room with Happy Birthday pink foil balloons, golden metallic latex balloons, and many other items to celebrate your birthday with pomp and show; you shall wear a birthday dress; and we all shall give you sweet kisses, and shower you the blessings for long life and prosperity."

"Uncle, please don't forget to get a cute 'teddy bear' and a chocolate box; and I shall distribute the chocolates to all those present in the room." Abhimanyu exclaimed with joy by clapping his hands in appreciation.

Haji Rasool provided Jai Koul with a rent free guest house in the backyard of his house. He took Abhimanyu to a psychiatrist; and as per the advice of the doctor, arranged the admission of little Abhimanyu in a day-boarding play-way school within few days. He also helped Jai Koul in establishing a business in the town to earn a livelihood!

Abhimanyu showed fast signs of recovery, and was fully recovered within a few months. The life of Jai Koul and his family was back on rails, and Haji Rasool was an angel in the form of a man for his family!

Jai Koul, though well settled in Khajoraho, is yearning to go back to his roots!

> *"It is incredible that this must be said, but the obvious seems to escape politicized academics, so we must state the obvious: Genocide is deliberate; it is premeditated. There is no genocide without premeditation. The murderers are not unfortunate coincidences. This is why it is called 'Mass MURDER' and not mass MANSLAUGHTER."*
>
> **– A.E. Samaan.**

6

Inherent Determined Resilience of Nandni, The Brave Hearted Lady

Nand Lal was born in a well-to-do family in a far-flung village of 'Breng *pargana*', in south Kashmir. During his school life, he enjoyed spending his leisure time collecting smooth cobbles from the riverbeds of 'River Brengi', and loved to hear stories of precious gemstones and history of gems.

After completing his Masters in geology; Nand Lal was appointed a junior geologist in the geology and mining department of the state; and assigned the task of work-planning for the extraction of sapphire in Paddar mining sites of Kishtwar in J&K. He was married to Nandni, the lone daughter of Dina Nath, the renowned landlord of '*kutt'har pargana*' in south Kashmir.

From a young age, Nand Lal craved for living an aristocratic life-style, and had a strong desire to do and experience something greater in life. His cherished wish was to make a quick buck, and that prompted him to leave the job of junior geologist voluntarily in early 70's. After having decided to start a secretive sapphire-business, Nand Lal paid frequent visits to the Paddar area to get connected with the people engaged in the clandestine collection of sapphire gems from dug out places, rockslide locations, creeks and streams in the areas adjacent to sapphire extraction sites.

Nand Lal often visited Jaipur, the gem-cutting capital of India, for faceting and polishing rough gems; and developed a bond of friendship with Gopal, who was running the family business of gemstone cutting in the city.

Nand Lal's secretive gem-business flourished in a few years, and he made a fortune. In the year 1986, while he was trekking along the mountainside road in Kishtwar area, a boulder hit him in a sudden rockslide, and both his legs were fractured. He was admitted to a hospital for nearly one month, and Nandni, his wife, remained at his bedside. Nand Lal's lower limbs developed gangrene, and his condition became critical with each passing day.

While in hospital, with dying breaths and glossy eyes, he whispered to Nandni, "Where have you kept my walking stick?" She brought the walking stick, and Nand Lal opened his eyes. Directing his gaze at Nandni's face, he said, "I gift this priceless walking stick to you. Keep it safely in your custody. My trusted friend, Gopal, knows its monetary value, and you can trust him too. Remember, it is a priceless stick." Instantly, he made a guttural noise and breathed his last.

Lone son of his father, Nand Lal was a dynamo. He inherited huge ancestral property including cultivable land, fruit orchards and a 4-story mansion. His wife, Nandni, was also the lone heir of her father; and she inherited the entire movable and immovable property of her father after his death in 1987.

Nandni was financially independent, and after the death of her husband, she kept the family together under one roof. Her four sons shared the joint responsibility of looking after the domestic affairs of the extended family; and every member of her family lived a happy and contented life, and they shared their joys and sorrows with each other.

After the death of her husband, Nandni's joint familial ship sailed smoothly for more than three years. As the nature's scheme of things is unanticipated, Nandni was unaware of a catastrophe befalling her family. Her family was driven into wandering around the dark fog of uncertainties of life after the unexpected turn of events in Kashmir valley, in January, 1990. She and her family members were coerced to leave the land of their ancestors. Nandni, along with her family members, left her home empty-handed, and all that she carried with her were the nostalgic memories of her homeland and a walking stick, with a stag horn handle, gifted to her by her husband, minutes before his death.

After abandoning the home and hearth, under compelling circumstances, Nandni's family reached Jammu; and the struggle for survival of the joint family began in a new environment.

A camp had been established in Gole-pully area of Jammu, for providing temporary shelter to internally displaced Kashmiri Pandits who were coerced to flee from their homeland. Nandni and Satesh, her unmarried son, were accommodated in a tent; and next to them, Autar and Sohan, her two married sons, were allotted two separate tents. Badri, the eldest son of Nandni, was provided shelter by his local friend in a quarter of domestic employees, in Bhori area of Talab Tiloo.

On the eve of *Maha Shiv Ratri*, Nandni was soothing her mind and soul during her morning prayers in one of the corners of the tent, and Satesh left for defecation in open fields near the tented camp. On his return, he tripped over the guy-cord of the tent, and hurt his rib cage badly. He was rushed to Medical College Hospital in a horse driven cart. His thorough medical checkup revealed that he had suffered a fracture in rib. He was kept under observation by a consultant for about two hours; and discharged from the hospital with advice to restrict body movements, besides prescribing medication which included icing the hurt area. He was brought to his tented-home, and despairing Nandni, in a flood of tears, got busy giving him ice pack therapy.

Around the time of Satesh's fall in tented shelter-home, Badri's residence had been engulfed in a fire due to a kerosene-stove burst, and everything in his quarter had been consumed by the flames; and Nandni and other members of her family were oblivious of the incident.

At around noon, frightened and dejected Badri, his wife and their two siblings, Rohit and Priya, showed up at her tented residence. Wailing Badri narrated to her mother the horrible experience, and shocked Nandni consoled them one by one. To comfort Badri, she said, "Badri, good and bad things do happen in life, don't you feel downhearted. You must remember that bright sun appears over the horizon after a dark night!" Escaping the attention of Badri and his family, she came out of the tent; and with tearful eyes, looked towards the sky and said, "O' Lord Shiva, do you want to test my power of endurance by sending me all the misfortunes, one after another?"

The weather in the temporary shelter home was dark and gloomy, and the faces of Nandni's family members presented a gloomy picture too. As soon as the storm started blowing in the tented area with long sound and rustling of tree leaves, 6-year old Priya came running and sat in the lap of her granny. Nandni gazed at her face; pictured memories of cradling Priya in arms and narrating fairy tales and Kashmiri rhymes to her; and with trembling lower lip, tears stung her eyes. Never before had Priya seen the eyes of her granny filled with tears, and she said to her innocently, "*Daadi Ma*, What happened? Today is '*Hearath*'; don't you know that shedding tears on this day is inauspicious?

"I am in pain and agony." Nandni murmured while kissing her cheeks.

"Why are you in pain and agony?" Little Priya asked.

"You can't understand that." Nandni replied, with a sigh.

"Why can't I understand?" Priya said curiously.

"I miss the extended familial structure and the interwoven culture of Kashmiri Pandits very badly" Nandni replied, with a flood of tears.

Nandni tried to look brave; and with an artificial smile, she said, "How do you know today is Shiv-Ratri?"

"I know it is 'Hearath' today, Papa and Mummy were talking about it for the last so many days. Isn't *Hearath* the same as S*hivratri*?" Priya asked.

"Yes, it is S*hivratri* today, we call it *Hearath* in our homeland, Kashmir; and Hearath is the festival of our traditional values, cultural, religious ethos and mythologized past." Nandni replied, with a smile.

"Why do we celebrate this festival?"Curious Priya asked.

"We celebrate *Hearath* festival for our spiritual upliftment, moral enrichment and soul purification. The festival is spread over 23 days; and the unique festival adds substance, strength, warmth and spiritual color to us." Nandni replied.

Slumped in dejection, Nandni's family members including her sons, listened to the conversation between her and Inquisitive little Priya, with focus and attention. After Priya fell asleep in the lap of her grandmother, Nandni chose to imbibe positivity in her sons, and said, "The creative power of 'Paramashiva' is 'Parvati', 'Uma' or 'Shakti'; the life has always been going on and will go on endlessly till dissolution; and we, the human beings, have to keep moving forward and adapt to emerging situations."

Organized around the family, the three married sons of Nandni, Badri, Autar and Sohan, were living an affluent life in Kashmir valley, but after leaving their homeland, they were unable to find a way even to achieve a small measure of their earlier lifestyles in an alien environment. Loss of privacy in tented homes irked them continually.

Nandni's sons put their heads together and decided to go to construct three residential houses; and succeeded in motivating Nandni to sell the immovable property of her father. Nandni executed the sale deed of orchards and agricultural land to a buyer at a throwaway price; and her three married sons shared the sale proceeds. Badri, Autar and Sohan utilized the money for the construction of three duplex houses in the city of Jammu.

Nandni's three sons shifted to their houses, and Nandni along with her unmarried son, Satesh, shifted to one-room tenement, allotted to her by the government in Mishriwala camp, located on the outskirts of Jammu.

Measured in units, 'time' never stops, and nobody can stop time. Nandni's family was split into four small units; each member of the family started contributing exclusively to the well-being of his or her own family-unit. The quality and frequency of the communication between the extended family members diminished gradually; and the bond that existed among the children of the extended family started eroding fast.

Nandni's youngest son Satesh, after recovering from the rib-cage injury was engulfed by depression; and was neglected by his brothers. Nandni's heart bled to see her sons deviating from the humanistic way of earlier life which held ethics and morals at the forefront of everything; and she watched everything helplessly. The frequency of visits by the sons to their mother's place also came down with each day passing by.

Even after Nandni's sons shifted to their new homes, they were not happy because they rudely displaced had no resources to enjoy the luxurious privileges they were used to in the land of their ancestors. They had an immense desire of living a finer and grandiose life. To live a life of style, they decided to sell their ancestral property in Kashmir. They persuaded Nandni and Satesh to sign the sale deed by offering to construct a separate house for them, adjacent to their houses. The trio spent the cash received from the sale of the immovable assets of joint family to live lavish lifestyle until they spent every penny. They duped their old mother and sick brother without feeling guilty.

Nandni subsisted on government's inadequate dole in the form of ration and meager relief-money. She was advancing in years, and her son, Satesh, was suffering from somatic system disorder, and she was reduced to poverty and despair. The mother-son duo was having a tough time in a migrant camp. Neither Nandni nor his son were able to earn; and Nandni sold her golden ornaments including the 'Dej-hor', a dangling ear ornament worn by Kashmiri Pandit women, to meet the medical expenses of her ailing son. Her sons had bidden bye to values of joint family and kinship.

One fine morning, while Nandni was busy serving '*Nun-Chai*', salty pink tea, and '*phulka*', home-made flat bread made of wheat flour, to Satesh at the breakfast time, a crow, sitting near the window of her one-room-tenement, started crowing, and she said to Satesh, "See, this mad crow is indicating the arrival of a guest to our place. How are we going to entertain him?" Satesh took a deep sigh and said, "Trust in God; let everybody including our near and dear ones fall away; God shall come at the appropriate time to pull us out of mire".

Satesh's words 'God shall come at the appropriate time to pull us out of mire' echoed in Nandni's mind, and she heard somebody knocking at the gate. She opened the door, and was surprised to find Gopal and his wife, from Jaipur, standing at the gate. They had last visited and stayed in Nandni's grand residential house in Kashmir valley in the year 1987, after the death of Nand Lal. She welcomed the guests to the one-room tenement. Gopal and his wife were astonished to find Satesh lying on a *khatiya*, a rope-bed, in one of the corners of the room, and the small multipurpose room used as the drawing room, the kitchen, the dining room and the bed room. Reminiscing on the good days of her past lifestyle, they were shocked and muted to see the pathetic condition of Nandni.

Although overwhelming incidents had made Nandni sad, and her face was gloomy, yet she felt delighted and happy to see Gopal and his wife. She exhibited the highest standards of generosity and friendly treatment to both, and served them a big breakfast.

An informal interaction between the guests and Nandni started, and Satesh looked put out and seemed completely unconcerned because he was suffering from mental health disorder. The woeful tale of exodus and chain of events that unfolded during the period of exile of Nandni made Gopal and his wife weep bitterly. While the interaction between Nandni and her guests continued, Gopal said," Nandni Bhabi, where have you kept late Nand lal's 'walnut walking cane with a Stag-horn handle'?"

"The 'walnut walking cane with a Stag-horn handle' is a souvenir, a precious gift, an item of sentimental value, for me. I lost everything except that." Nandni said, with eyes filled with tears.

"Thank God." Gopal said, joyfully.

Gopal was Nand Lal's most trustworthy friend. Nand Lal shared everything to Gopal; and Gopal was privy to designing and fabrication of the 'walking cane'; and Gopal knew that the walking cane' was not a mere cane, but a hidden treasure. He wanted to see the 'walking cane', and asked Nandni to show him the cane. At the instance of Gopal, Nandni drew out the walking stick from a CGI trunk and placed before Gopal.

Gopal detached the Stag-horn handle from the walnut-wood shaft; using a screw driver for unscrewing the double hinged cover of the stag-horn handle, and took out 20 precious Sapphire gems that were concealed in the cavity; and presented the precious gems to Nandni. Simultaneously, Gopal said to Nandni, "Nand Lal once said to me: Gopal, I have had very good days with my wife; I want to gift her something unique; and if I die before her, I don't want her to see bad days." After hearing this, Nandni and Gopal's wife burst into tears.

The mother-son duo left for Jaipur In the company of Gopal and his wife in the evening. At Jaipur, Satesh was admitted to a renowned psychiatric hospital, and he recovered fully. Gopal used his expertise in marketing the gem stones after Nandni consented; and the sale proceeds fetched her lakhs of rupees. She purchased a two-bedroom flat in the outskirts of Jaipur; deposited a portion of money in the bank; and that fetched her recurring monthly income to sustain.

Gopal engaged Satesh in his ancestral business of gem-cutting; and within few months, he married his daughter to Satesh.

The marriage function of Satesh was attended by all the erstwhile members of the extended family of Nandni. Immutably driven by the maternal instinct, she had personally visited Jammu to invite all; with the sole object of piecing the relationship together, she delivered mother's sermon to all the members of her erstwhile joint family. She addressed them passionately: "Nobody knows the God's will, obvious or hidden; whatever happened all these years or is likely to happen in future is the will of God; and nobody must harbor grudges against any of his tormentors, be he a Kashmiri Muslim neighbor or the own kith and kin, because that is not going to ease the pain, but that shall multiply the unpleasant feelings."

Destiny presented the toughest and challenging circumstances of bearing the pain of disintegration of an extended family to Nandni. Away from home and hearth, Nandni's happiness was blotted out and buried overnight, but the brave-hearted lady kept hanging on; struggled to her optimum; endured the pain; and did not bend till her end. She experienced the compelling experiences of life!

> *"Exile is strangely compelling to think about but terrible to experience. It is the unhealable rift forced between a human being and a native place, between the self and its true home: its essential sadness can never be surmounted. And while it is true that literature and history contain heroic, romantic, glorious, even triumphant episodes in an exile's life, these are no more than efforts meant to overcome the crippling sorrows of estrangement."*
>
> **– Edward W. Said**

7

Tricked and Robbed Internally Displaced Persons

With booming thunder and plenty of lightning, it rained for about two hours in the Santra-mohr area of Talab-tiloo on *Raksha Bandhan* Day-2005, and after the downpour stopped, children came out of their homes to have fun and frolic in a small park. In a few minutes, a snake-charmer, carrying two small baskets, hanging from a bamboo stick, slung over his shoulders, also got there. He sat on the green turf in the corner of the park; and about fifty people, young and old, thronged the park to watch his skills within minutes. The snake charmer took the lid off the basket; and started playing *Pungi,* a flute-like Indian musical instrument. A cobra snake raised his head and neck almost straight up from the basket and after assuming the standing posture, started moving his hood with the snake charmer's swaying movements of the *Pungi.*

While the snake charmer was busy enticing the snake with sound vibrations of Pungi to swing the raised portion of his body in a rhythmic way, Pushkar Raina, a respectable person of the area, asked him to ensure that the deadly cobra did not go berserk and bite the young spectators, who were sitting very close to baskets. Snake charmer perceived that Pushkar's behavior was insulting, and he gazed at Pushkar with a sneering look. An impulsive exchange of hot words ensued between the two; and snake charmer threw verbal tantrums of worst kind at Pushkar. Pushkar shouted at him to get lost. The enraged snake-charmer set loose the two snakes from the baskets, and left the spot. The children were terrified to see snakes crawling in the park; and they ran helter-skelter.

Santra-mohr area of Talab-tiloo was mostly inhabited by the turfed out Kashmiri Hindus from their homeland. In their newfound places of shelter, many of them were bitten by snakes, a most uncommon thing in their homeland; and after finding two venomous snakes set loose by their handler, the displaced persons, living near the park, were panic-stricken.

Soon after the snake charmer abandoned the pair of snakes, three persons, attired in yellow robes, typical of *Sadhus*, reached the park area. The eldest, aged about sixty, sported a beard and long dreadlocks; and the other two, in their mid thirties, were clean-shaven, wearing yellow turbans. The elder *Sadhu* laid eyes on Pushkar Raina, and said, "I find the people startled, is everything alright here?" Thinking that the trio was beggars in the garb of *Sadhus*, Pushkar gave him a scorching look, and did not reply. Pushkar's deliberate silence irritated the *Sadhu*, and he said, "Mind it that we are neither beggars nor are we in search of food, offerings and alms, and take note of the fact that we are archaic *Sadhus*, not beggars; and remember that showing disrespect to a *Sadhu* is reprehensible." Pushkar stared at him and gave a brief account of all that had happened, hesitatingly though.

The *Sadhu* offered his help to rid the inhabitants of the scare by catching the deadly snakes, and Pushkar said, "We shall be grateful, but won't allow anyone to kill the snakes."

"We are not snake charmers; we know how to catch them alive; and in doing that, even if they bite us, we will not be harmed." *Sadhu* replied with a charming smile.

While seizing alive the snakes with bare hands, a cobra snake raised his body straight off the ground and stung the hand of the elder *Sadhu* with his fang. Although blood drops trickled down his hand yet, he took hold of the cobra snake in a carefree manner. The snakes were caught alive; and the *Sadhus* put them in two cloth bags for releasing in a forested area. The people living in Santra Mohr area felt relaxed after getting rid of the two venomous snakes. They were however surprised to see the *Sadhu* unharmed after he was bitten by a Cobra.

The elder *Sadhu* was offered money by the inhabitants, but he refused to accept it; and, shaking his head, he said, "I am a *Sanyasi* and I don't need money, possessions and comforts of life". After a great deal of persuasion by Pushkar Raina, the trio consented to have d*al-r*ice meals at the residence of Meera, an elderly lady living next to the park.

After their coerced exodus from homeland, Hindu minority population of Kashmir took refuge in various parts of the country. Among the lakhs of Kashmiri Hindus, driven out by design, Meera's husband, Bushan lal, was also a victim of human displacement. He was forced to live in the scorching heat and humid climate in a new environment; resultantly, he suffered a sun-stroke; and had been suffering from severe physical deficits including speech disorder for many years.

After the elder *Sadhu* entered the residential house of Meera, he found sick Bushan lal lying in bed. He gave a gentle pat on his face. Looking intently into *Sadhu's* eyes, tears trickled down the face of Bushan lal; and the *Sadhu* said, "*Maha-Dev* will bless you!"

Meera was frustrated and upset for many years. She was susceptible to trying and believing anything and everything to see her husband recovering from prolonged illness. Shedding tears and drying her eyes with the *Saree* she was wearing, Meera bent on her knees, touched the *Sadhu's* feet and said, "*Baba Ji*, I feel the positive energy of your divine power; and you have sanctified my house and surroundings." Moving his tongue across his lips, *Sadhu* focused his eyes over the fast rotating ceiling fan for about a minute; and in a sedate tune, he said to Meera, "The only treatment that can cure him is '*Pooja*' and '*Anushthan*'; you need to perform '*Swarn sidhi-Anushthan'*; and if the '*Pooja*' is performed strictly according to ancient texts, the sick person will be perfectly alright within days."

"Will he recover fully, *Baba Ji*?" Meera said impatiently, with tears in her eyes.

"Yes; with the blessings of my Guru, he will be alright within days." *Sadhu* replied.

"Baba ji, please tell me how and where '*Swarn sidhi-Anushthan*' is performed?" Curious Meera asked.

"The a*nushthan* i*s* performed at two places simultaneously–in the house of the sick person and on the River bank; and the *Pooja* is consecrated only if performed by a learned Brahmin priest or a *Sanyasi* having thorough knowledge about *Tantra*." *Sadhu* replied.

Meera did hear from the *Sadhu* what she wanted to, and accepted his words as true. *Sadhu's* words triggered positive reactions in Meera; and details of joy over Meera's face enchanted the people in attendance. Meera, her relatives including Pushkar Raina, the elder brother of her husband, and her friends expressed keenness to go for *Pooja* and *anushthan* immediately. With folded hands, Pushkar Raina said to *Sadhu*, "*Baba Ji*, We want to start the *Pooja* as early as possible."

After the trio took a meal of rice and *dal* at Meera's residence, the elder *Sadhu* made the significant features of 'a*nushthan'* clear to everybody present there. Pushkar Raina noted down the list of accoutrements of religious ritual, which included two medium sizes '*Kalasha* metal pots', two red-color cloth pieces and two thick plastic ropes. While dictating the list of accoutrements of '*anushthan*', *Sadhu* laid emphasis on fetching two '*Kalasha* metal pots' of the same dimension and size with large base and small mouth.

The next morning, as already decided, *Sadhus* reached Meera's house for *Pooja* ritual. Accouterments of the *Pooja* ritual were laid out near the bed of sick Bushan lal. Elder *Sadhu* blew the conch shell, and started the ritual by reciting the hymns and offering the material in a small lit fire, and the practice continued for nearly three hours.

Amid the *Pooja* ritual, the elder *Sadhu* said to Pushkar, "Beginning today, we shall hold three sessions of *Pooja* on alternate days, but after the conclusion of *Pooja* of the last session, you shall have to serve meals to about one hundred hungry people; and with the blessings of *Bholay Nath Ji,* the sick person will be in a position to serve the food."

"Arranging food for one hundred people is no big deal; we can arrange meals for five hundred people." Pushkar replied with a smile.

"Amidst chanting of Vedic hymns, we have to waive currency notes over the head of the sick person to rid him off from evil spirits; and the same currency notes shall be spent by you for arranging and offering meals to hungry people." *Sadhu* said.

Pushkar deputed his son to go to a nearby branch of the bank, and within a few minutes, he brought two fresh packs of Rupees ten thousand each and placed before the *Sadhu*. The *Sadhu* applied the vermilion paste to one of the *Kalasha* pots; and, amidst chanting of hymns, after waiving over the head of sick Bushan Lal, all the 200 currency notes of Rs 100 denomination were put into the pot.

The elder Sadhu gave sermons about the significance of '*Swarn sidhi-Anushthan*' to about 30-35 people in attendance at the residential house of Meera. "There are negative energies and bad spirits in almost every house which create problems for inmates; people fall sick and do not recover despite medical treatment; the smooth flow of life is hampered; and if the negative energies and bad spirits are not cleared, it makes life a living hell. People are ignorant of the fact that wearing golden ornaments and gemstones without prescribed *Pooja* generally attract negative energies; and before wearing, the golden ornaments need to be activated by performing *Swarn sidhi* Pooja. '*Swarn sidhi-Anushthan*', the most potent of all to cure an ailing person, includes the Gold-pooja ritual", the Sadhu said.

The *Sadhu* invited the inmates to place the golden ornaments worn by them in the said *Kalasha*-pot for p*ooja*. The family members and relatives of sick Bushan Lal complied and put the golden ornaments in to the pot amidst chanting of Vedic hymns. The ornaments included golden rings, chains, bracelets and the '*Dejhoors*', an ornament worn by Kashmiri Pandit women. The *Sadhu* put a lid on the pot; wrapped the pot, containing money and gold ornaments in red-color cloth; secured the lid by fastening the cloth with the neck of the pot, using a thin rope; and entrusted the pot to Meera for safe custody.

After the *Pooja* ritual at the residence of Meera, the *Sadhus* left for *Pooja* near the embankment of River Tawi with the empty '*Kalasha*-pot' and a little portion of the *Pooja* material. While leaving, elder *Sadhu* instructed Meera to keep the *Kalash*-pot containing cash and golden ornaments in the steel almirah, and cautioned her to be aware of thieves and burglars.

As per schedule, the elder *Sadhu* along with one of his juniors visited Meera's house early morning on day-3 to resume the *Pooja*. The duo had brought with them the other *Kalasha*-pot and accouterments in a bag for p*ooja* ritual near the river bank. On the instruction of the elder *Sadhu*, the *Mandap* for p*ooja* was relocated to the adjoining room because circumambulations of the sick person needed more space in the room where the sick was lying on the bed. The elder *Sadhu* lit the fire in the adjoining room, *and* entrusted the job of *Pooja*, offerings and chanting of hymns to his junior. *Kalasha-pot* wrapped in red-color cloth, containing cash and gold ornaments, was placed near the *Pooja Mandap,* and the junior *Sadhu* started the *Pooja.* The elder *Sadhu* invited the people in attendance for circumambulations of the sick person around his bed; and amidst chanting of hymns by the *Sadhu*, everybody present in the house joined the ritual, with eyes closed, as directed.

After the circumambulations of sick Bushan Lal who lay on the bed, the elder *Sadhu* instructed Meera to keep the '*Kalasha-pot*', lying near the *Mandap,* in the steel almirah, which she complied with. He also instructed her to ensure that the oil lamp was reinforced with oil lest it be extinguished before the conclusion of the final schedule of the ritual. With a view to keeping the confidence level of the inmates high, he reassured them that before the onset of the final session of the p*ooja*, they would get to see the miracle, and the sick person shall leave the bed and join the p*ooja*. An *aarti*, recitation of hymns in unison by the participants, was performed by the elder *Sadhu*; and the duo left for the ritual near the bank of river with an assurance of coming back after a day for leading the ritual to fruition.

Meera and her relatives and friends were optimistic; they expected that a miracle was likely to happen; and the waiting weighed heavy on their minds. They impatiently waited for the S*adhus* to come on the scheduled day and time, but they did not turn up till noon.

Meera did not give up the hope, and waited until it was dark. The date and time for performing the last and final session of *Pooja* on day-5 had already been decided by the S*adhus*, but they did not show up even after 24 hours of the scheduled day and time.

Meera's relatives and neighbors had no clue of the temporary abode of *Sadhus* in the city or elsewhere. After waiting for two days, a group of people from the area left for a look out of *Sadhus* in and around the city, but their efforts were in vain. Finally, it was decided to wait for one more day for opening the *Kalasha-pot* so that the gold ornaments could be returned to their respective owners.

After a long wait of three days, the *Kalasha-pot* was drawn from the steel almirah and Pushkar Raina unfastened the rope from the neck of the pot, and removed the red-color cloth. After removing the lid of the *Kalasha* pot, he was dumbstruck to find the glimpse of a cobra snake; and he quickly slammed the lid of the pot.

A snake catcher was called in to remove and relocate the snake. After observing the snake minutely, the snake catcher told the men in attendance that the snake was harmless as his fangs and venom-glands had been removed. The snake was removed from the pot by the snake catcher, and Meera and her relatives were rattled after he inverted the pot. They didn't believe their eyes what they saw–instead of golden ornaments and currency notes, twenty odd pebbles fell on the floor from the pot. They kept looking at each other in surprise.

Astonished Meera said to Pushkar, "How did they do that?"

"We have been defrauded by an organized group of criminals, masquerading as ascetics, and I am sure that the snake charmer and the fake Sadhus were working closely towards a common goal."Disgusted Pushkar said in a feeble voice.

"But, how did they replace the golden ornaments and the currency notes with pebbles." Meera asked.

"They did it on day-3 of the p*ooja,* when the elder *Sadhu* invited us for circumambulations of the sick person around his bed; and all of us joined the ritual, with eyes closed. The junior

Sadhu substituted the pot containing cash and golden ornaments with a similar type of pot, filled with the pebbles and cobra snake, which had been brought in a bag; and they left with the pot containing cash and gold." Pushkar said, heaping bitter and abusive language on fraudsters.

A gang of notorious criminals, masquerading as *Sadhus* and snake charmers, succeeded in fooling and tricking the gullible. In an uncontrollable outburst of emotions, Meera started beating her breast and crying aloud: "We have been ruined financially by the greedy people, both at home and in exile." Pushkar cupped his face in his hands and groaned: "We have been harmed physically, emotionally and economically too; we have been living as refugees in our own country for the last fifteen years because the political dispensations at Centre and the politicians of Kashmir are trading business and earning profits by exploiting us in forced wandering; and in desperation, we have become vulnerable; and the criminals and masqueraders prey on us."

> *"In every age it has been the tyrant, the oppressor and the exploiter who has wrapped himself in the cloak of patriotism, or religion, or both to deceive and overawe the people."*
>
> **– Eugene Victor Debs**

8

Topsy-Turvy KPs in Exile

On November 07, 1980, *Amavasya* of the month of *Kartik,* the *Diwali*-day, Roshan Lal and his wife, Indirani, were busy making *Rangoli* near the entrance door of their residential house to welcome the goddess of good fortune and prosperity, *Lakhshmi.* Suddenly, Indirani, who was eight months pregnant, suddenly developed severe pregnancy complications, and Roshan Lal rushed her to a maternity hospital. As the male attendants of the patients were not allowed into the labor cum recovery ward, Indrani's husband was denied entry by the gatekeeper.

Disgusted Roshan Lal sat down on a wooden bench, built around the trunk of a Chinar tree, on the lawns of the maternity hospital. Looking skywards, the magnificent beauty of the changed colour of the leaves of elegant Chinar tree, from green to crimson, anchored Roshan Lal to nostalgic feelings of sweet memories of his meetings and love-romance courtship days with Indirani under a similar Chinar tree in Naseem Bagh, in the outskirts of Srinagar city. Tears started to trickle down his cheeks. After few minutes, he saw his wife being carried by two attendants of the maternity home on a wheeled stretcher towards the operation theatre for an emergency surgical procedure; and he followed the wheeled stretcher. He was again stopped by a paramedic from going beyond the gangway that linked the operation theatre gate. After signing the consent form for the surgical procedure of his wife, he sat down on a steel bench.

To get an update on the surgery of his wife, Roshan Lal anxiously waited for somebody to step out from the operation theatre; and the long wait made him chew his fingernails literally to the bone. The suspense continued for nearly two hours until a doctor came out of the operation theatre. The Doctor stared into his eyes, and with a gesture of 'Thumbs-up', he said to Roshan Lal, "Good luck!" Although the smiling words of the doctor delivered a high dose of positivity to him yet he was eager to know whether his wife had delivered a male or female child.

After some time, a female nurse exited from the operation theatre; and Roshan Lal ran after her, with bated breath, to enquire about the new born child as also the condition of his wife. He got to know that his wife had delivered triplets, two males and a female. Upon getting the surprising information from the female Nurse, Roshan Lal looked dumbfounded. He was lost in thoughts, and the question that lurked at the back of his mind was: 'How could Indirani cater to the requirements of all the three neonates?'He cupped his face in his hands to visualize the impending problems; and made repeated efforts to peep through the tinted-glass partition of neonatal intensive care to have a glimpse of the triplets, but in vain.

Distraught with anxiety, Roshan Lal decided to give the female neonate to one of his close friends for upbringing. The childless Ashok and his wife Sheila, both working as teachers in a government-school, expressed their willingness to adopt the female neonate on the condition of maintaining confidentiality. The biological parents of the neonate, made a solemn promise that they would, in no circumstance, let any other person know about it, and never confide to the female neonate at any stage of her life; and the care and custody of the neonate was given to Ashok and Sheila secretly.

Residents of the civil lines area of Srinagar city, Roshan lal was a practicing lawyer and his wife, a teacher, working in a public school; and Ashok and his wife Sheila were their neighbors.

After two years, one of the two male toddlers, Mohan, was adopted by Damodhar, his maternal grandfather, who, In search of brighter economic opportunities, had migrated from Kashmir and settled in New Delhi in the early 70s.

Mohan and Rohan possessed all human potentialities to develop under favorable social conditions, and nature and nurture was in favor of both. They were admitted to two reputed day-boarding schools on their fourth birth-day, Mohan in New Delhi and Rohan in Kashmir valley; and both embarked on the journey of life to grow and to shape their future.

Towards the beginning of 1990, the valley of Kashmir was completely rocked by terror attacks; and the violent actions and threats were meticulously designed to coerce the minuscule religious minority of Kashmir to flee from their homeland. The family members of Roshan Lal, including little Rohan, and Ashok and his wife Sheila, along with their 1o-year old adopted daughter, left their homeland for destinations unknown in the month of March 1990.

The inescapable fate turned cruel for Rohan after the exodus of his parents from the land of their ancestors. He got trapped in an existential crisis. Affluent lifestyle of Roshan Lal had changed overnight, and his dream of achieving the developmental milestones of Rohan was shattered into a million pieces. The changed environment in a new habitat came in the way of shaping character, caliber and future of Rohan according to the plans of his father; and he was admitted to a government school. Under compelling circumstances, little Rohan was forced to abandon the best of his past and to blend with a new set of friends.

Rohan endured the emotional trauma of the loss of home and the separation from his classmates, friends and acquaintances, and related himself to the new world in a short period of time. The brilliant boy adapted to the situation in which he was thrown by circumstances, and quickly learned to speak the language of the place where he had settled anew.

Within a few months, the culture and other aspects of life in new environment impacted Rohan's fragile mind; and a perceptible attitudinal and behavioral change in him became easy to catch sight of. His nonphysical traits began to deviate gradually, and he lost interest in playing the piano which he once liked the most to play for hours.

Roshan Lal was struggling to find his feet in the new environment to achieve a small measure of the earlier lifestyle. In the hope of returning to his roots, he waited for two years in the most distressing and trying times without any respite; and later, joined the bar in a civil court.

Although the parents of little Rohan had been observing that he was becoming defiant and ill-mannered, neglecting relationships and reacting negatively yet they could not figure out the reason for the metamorphosis and his rapidly changing behavior. Much water had flowed down the River Jhelum for five long years, but Roshan Lal and Indirani were incognizant of the routines and transitions of their son, Rohan.

On a hot and humid day of July, 1995, Rohan's mother found a sharp edged knife, a pouch of cannabis and a bundle of currency notes in his school bag, and she took the items in her possession. Rohan assaulted and beat her for reclaiming the items. Roshan Lal had no inkling of the fact that Rohan had been driven into drug-selling and becoming a drug addict. He was shocked to find himself sunk in apathy after an emotionally disturbed Indirani revealed to him the ugly incident and he advised her to stay calm and avoid outbursts of emotions and getting angry.

In the month of September, 1995, Rohan was shifted to Delhi and admitted to a drug de-addiction centre where he remained for six months. He lost two precious academic years; and after resuming academics, Rohan graduated with a degree in Information Technology. He became a freelance TV Producer; and produced a 30-minute documentary film on 'Exodus of miniscule minority from Kashmir' and started boastfully introducing himself, with all the eloquence and flamboyant gestures, as a show business personality at every social gathering.

While Rohan's parents were busy checking the background and matching the horoscope of a prospective bride, in typical Kashmiri Pandit tradition of arranged marriage, to tie Rohan in a nuptial lock, he confided to his mother that he had decided to remain a bachelor. In a fit of anger, Rohan arrogantly said to his mother, "Remember, I am to live life in my own style, without anybody's interference, and don't be under the impression that I shall dance to the tunes of my father and mother."

After their exodus from Kashmir, Ashok and Sheila along with their adopted daughter, Radha, lived in rented accommodation near the residential house of Mohan's family in New Delhi, but neither Mohan nor Radha knew that they were biological brother-sister; and whenever they met by chance, they would formally greet each other. After his PG Diploma in Film and Television, Mohan had established his film business and shifted to Noida.

After the drug addiction recovery, Rohan's parents made him follow a structured day; and Rohan attended morning yoga classes without fail. One day, he came across a young girl in the Yoga centre; the girl mistook Rohan as Mohan because he looked like him. She smilingly greeted Rohan, and a conversational interaction ensued between the two. "My name is Radha; I have been attending morning 'Yoga classes' regularly for the last 5-6 years; through Yoga, I feel rejuvenated, eternally fresh, unfailing and completely happy; and I have come to this yoga centre for the first time." Radha said to Rohan.

"Who taught you 'Yoga'?" Rohan asked.

"My *Guru*; one and the only one in the world, my 'Master'; his serenity keeps surrounding me round the clock; and when I sit near him, his fragrance fills me and I feel throbbing." Radha replied.

"Is he around?" Curious Rohan asked.

"No, but I feel his presence everywhere and every time." Radha said, with a smile.

"He must be very smart?" Rohan asked, with a smile.

"Yes, smart in mind, quite infinite!" Radha replied.

"Are you married?" Rohan asked.

"NO!" Radha said, with laughter.

Radha's mannerism, straightforwardness, openness to feelings, facial expressions, and, above all, her attractiveness fascinated Rohan so much that he instantly made up his mind to marry her. After reaching his home, he told his mother that he had found a girl, and wanted to marry her; and that made her mother feel jubilant.

Rohan was anxious to put forward his offer of marriage to Radha. On the next day, at the instance of Rohan, Radha met him in a botanical park in New Delhi. Initiating the discourse, Radha smilingly said, "Rohan, I noticed your eyes sparkling when you were talking to me yesterday; I want to tell you something about myself. It's no secret, but I think you don't know."

"Please!" looking up at the blue sky, Rohan said curiously.

"I have lived the life of a drug-addict for four long years." Radha said instantly.

"Are you joking?" Rohan said, with an unsmiling face.

"No, I am not joking." Radha said instantly.

"Do you want to tell me that I am a drug addict?" Rohan said.

"Rohan, what happened? I am telling you the truth." Radha replied after closing her eyes for a few seconds.

"No, I think you are talking sarcastically; and you want to tell me indirectly that I am a drug addict." Rohan stammered nervously.

"Rohan, why should I do that? Believe me, I am telling you the truth." Radha replied smilingly.

"Where do you live at present?" Rohan asked.

"I live in the house of my parents, my father and mother died in a road accident six months ago; I have no brother, and no sister, no uncle or aunty. I am 'single.' Radha said, with tearful eyes.

"Will you marry me?" Looking towards the branches of a tree to avoid eye contact, Rohan asked.

"No." Radha replied bluntly.

"Why?" Rohan asked.

"Because I am completely settled, and my mind has become silent, centered and focused; and I don't want my mind to conquer me again to fall back on my old self." Radha replied.

"It is beyond my capacity to understand your philosophical reply; will be grateful if you make me to understand what exactly you mean to say." Rohan asked.

"Listen: My goal of life is to achieve consciousness of soul for which, I think, I have sprung into existence; I want to live a real happy life through self- realization, the true identity of God; and that is superior to all physical and mental pleasures!" Radha replied eloquently.

Rohan endorsed the words of Radha by saying "O, my God, you are extraordinary; and I must emulate you".

After the meeting, Rohan came back home; and told his mother that after reconsideration, he withdraws from his earlier decision of entering into wed-lock. He also revealed to his mother about his meeting with a girl, Radha, whose parents, Ashok and Sheila had died in a road accident. In the course of interaction, it took Indirani no time to figure out as to who 'Radha' was. She could feel the impact of the death of Ashok and Sheila on Radha's psyche; and she visualized the intense emotional shock Radha must have been passing through after her drastically altered world. Her eyes became damp; with quivering lips, she instantly grabbed Rohan and held him close to her chest, sobbing and wailing for few minutes.

After coming to know about the death of Ashok and Sheila, Advocate Roshan Lal and Indirani decided to break the solemn promise; and they left no stone unturned in tracing the whereabouts of Radha.

Indirani and Roshan Lal reached an *Ashram* on the outskirts of South Indian metropolis of Chennai, and found Radha sitting under the feet of a '*Guru*', wearing orange-colour apparel. She had been given a new name *Ananda*, the 'Bliss', by her '*Guru*'. After some time the *Guru* withdrew, and entrusted *Ananda* the job of holding a discourse with a large group of his disciples, and while dwelling on '*Trika* philosophy' and '*Shiv Sutra*' at length, she elaborated on the process of manifestation and of the dissolution of the universe. She dwelt on the growth of a wide variety of underground economic activities and the existing illegal markets of drug trade in the country.

Roshan Lal and Indirani, seated in the audience, listened to her speech, full of smart vocabulary, related words and phrases in English, and their eyes were damp when she said, “I was driven to hard drugs, you know why? OK, I will tell you: I wanted to meditate for self-realization; I expressed my desire to my classmate, a neighbor, Mohan. He conducted me to an elderly person where I was served ‘Marijuana’, a soft drug, and later I switched over to hard drugs. Don’t you ever taste a soft or hard drug; you shall be enticed to do that because this not only flourishes the underground economy of terrorists but makes you and your country sick.”

Radha’s words touched the deepest chords of her biological mother. Sobbing Indirani said to her husband, “Swami, today I realized that cultures, howsoever different, distinct and unique they are, can’t remain insular and circumscribed in an alien land.”

“I think surroundings have an impact on emotionally fragile and young people.” Roshan Lal said.

“Yes, but I think the family roots are squarely responsible if the sprawling buds develop irregularly, awkwardly and ungracefully.” Indirani said, regretfully.

“Today, I have grasped that initially the people take to harmful drugs either to manage difficult emotions and worries or to tide over a topsy-turvy situation, and subsequently they develop an obsession for the drug.” Roshan Lal replied.

“We, as parents of our siblings, must neither ridicule nor hate them, but passionately help them to stop compulsive seeking and using drugs.” Indirani said

“Now, please tell me how we are going to meet and interact with our daughter?” Roshan Lal asked.

“I think, we must drop the idea of meeting Radha because she shall feel disturbed and upset.” Indirani said.

Roshan Lal and Indirani decided against meeting their daughter, Radha, and both left with a heavy heart!

> *"People without knowledge of their past history, origin and culture are like a tree without roots."*
>
> **– Marcus Garvey**

9

...And She Died Craving, To Go to the Homeland

The winter capital of Jammu witnessed a massive influx of hounded out minuscule minority community members from Kashmir, In January, 1990. A number of shelter-camps were established by the state administration to provide temporary shelter to displaced people. One such camp was located in a vast strip of barren land with low lying bushes of multiple stems, on the outskirts of Jammu city, situated along the Jammu-Akhnoor highway. In the vicinity of the shelter-camp, a sizable population of laborers lived in the temporary brick structures constructed by a brick-kiln owner.

The work-force of the brick-kiln, who had migrated to Jammu, from various states of the country, on their own discretion and free will, to earn better wages in a congenial working atmosphere, lived merrily in the temporary structures, but for the displaced minority community members of Kashmir, who had been hounded out from their homeland, living in a shelter-camp was an unpleasant and overwhelmingly distressing experience. After the coerced eviction from their homeland, more than two years ago, the families were struggling to find their feet in a new environment, and were not able to even achieve a small measure of their earlier lifestyles.

They were leading a miserable life, as refugees, in their own country.

Although the displaced community members had eventually adapted to the hot and humid climate of their new settlement, yet many had fallen prey to sleep-disorders because of the messy situation in shelter tents. The privacy of the tent dwellers was badly affected as the family units, comprising parents, siblings and grandparents were compelled by the circumstances to live together in ten feet by ten feet space; and they used to loiter in open fields and near the Ranbir Canal even at midnight. After the construction of a one-room brick structures at the campsite, the exiled community members were shifted to one-room tenements.

It was a hot summer night in 1992. A young girl, asleep with her parents in one of the structures of the brick-kiln, was bitten by a deadly cobra snake, and she died on the way to hospital. The news spread like wild fire; and the occurrence caused utter panic, fear and confusion in the entire shelter-camp.

After the sunrise, Inderjeet engaged himself in removing a pile of bricks and stones, besides cutting the wild shrubs, the hiding place of snakes, near his one-room tenement. At around 9 am, due to prolonged physical exertion in scorching heat, Inderjeet abruptly fainted and fell to the ground. He developed cramps in his arms and legs, perhaps due to heatstroke, and breathed his last in less than an hour; and his sudden death cast a gloom in the entire shelter-camp.

30-year old Inderjeet was the son of Raj Nath, who had died a tragic death a year ago. Raj Nath was trolling around the shelter camp in the early morning, and was hit and crushed to death by a speeding tractor. Inderjeet's mother, Rajrani, could not cope with the grief of losing her spouse; and the trauma of the loss of her spouse and the trials and tribulations of exodus wreaked havoc with her emotional and physical health. A fortnight earlier, Rajrani had a fall, and fractured her ankle. Her limb was put in a cast, and she was unable to move.

Rajrani's late husband was a Petition Writer. She was the mother of three sons. Mohan Lal was the oldest; Inderjeet, the second oldest; and Bushan Lal, the youngest. Mohan Lal, a state government employee, was attached to the newly constituted migrant employee's cell, Jammu; Inderjeet was running a grocery shop on the outskirts of Srinagar city prior to the displacement of Hindus from the valley; and Bushan Lal was a merchant navy officer, working with a private company. Mohan Lal was married, and Rajrani lived in a joint family with her sons, before and after her displacement.

Mohan Lal, shifted the dead body of his younger brother, Inderjeet, to a nearby community hall for observing the religious rites and rituals; and inconsolably weeping and sobbing Rajrani was also shifted there. Hundreds of camp dwellers, relatives and friends thronged the community hall to console the bereaved family and catch the last glimpse of the deceased. Rajrani's sounds of crying and moaning echoed through the community hall continually.

Mohan Lal was floating in an ocean of despair, extremely upset. The loss of home, death of his father, physical and emotional disorder of his mother, and the circumstances leading to the sudden death of his loved brother and also the upsetting and surprising events of exodus, were lurking at the back of Mohan Lal's mind constantly. Seeing the dead body of his brother, Inderjeet, when laid upon the pyre for consigning to flames, was a shocking and draining experience for him. Distraught Mohan Lal shouted aloud: "I spit in the face of all the exploitative politicians at the national and state level, who lent strength to the fundamentalists and divisive forces in my homeland over the years, which led to the predicament of the peace loving aborigines of Kashmir."

After the cremation of the dead body on the embankment of the Ranbir canal near the shelter camp, the community hall presented a sorrowful look. Rajrani had been administered a sedative, and she was calm; and Mohani, the wife of Mohan Lal, was busy reciting the verses of the Bhagavad Gita.

At around 9 pm, Mohan Lal and his wife changed the floor-bed linens of Rajrani; cleaned her body, using a moist towel and sponges; placed the pillows against the wall for her comfortable sleep in a sitting-up posture; fed her with juice and biscuits; and engaged her in a light interaction to cheer her up.

Rajrani listened to her son and daughter-in-law calmly without any irritation or anguish for some time. She suddenly said to her son, "Mohana, who is looking after our apple, walnut and cherry trees in the village?" Without giving a pause, she said to Mohani, "Mohani, before we proceed to our village, we shall break our journey to visit *Lal Trag* Park, near Pampore, and sit and relax there for some time."

Rajrani was craving to return to her native village, longing to go back to her homeland. Her words evoked nostalgic and tender sentiments of Mohan Lal and other family members about the homeland of their forbears; and tears welled up in the eyes of all those present in the hall. In a blink, tired and exhausted Rajrani dozed off again.

Mohan Lal spread a bedsheet over a foam mattress on the floor, next to his mother; stretched his body over the bed, and closed his eyes to sleep. His thought process got activated instantly; and he started searching for the reply to many questions, lurking at the back of his mind for over two years, and the questions included: "Was the centuries-old cultural heritage of Kashmiri Pandits going to get lost in the pages of history; have the internally displaced members to fight the battle of return and resettlement in their homeland till they all perish one by one; and whether or not the community in exile shall rise to fight those who betrayed and led them to vicissitudes?"

Mohan Lal was awake for hours, and his mother, Rajrani, had transited into 'dream world', the realm of fantasy. Asleep in the sitting-up posture, Rajrani suddenly snapped out of the dream; gave a staggering push to Mohan Lal; intently looked at his face for a few seconds; and said, "*Mohana*, It has been snowing the whole day; more than 6 feet snow has accumulated over the shingled roof-top of our house; why don't you and Inderjeet clear the snow-load off the roof?" She again closed her eyes, and started snoring mildly.

It took Mohan Lal no time to grasp that Rajrani was half-awake, and she had travelled to her home in dreaming state, an altered consciousness. He gazed at her face, and watched a tuft of her hair move up and down on her face due to the moving air of a standing-fan. Abruptly, she woke up again, and while yawning and rubbing her eyes, she glanced over the surroundings, laughed in a loud and boisterous manner, and said to her son in a meek voice, "Are you my son, *Mohana*?"

"Yes, Mother." Mohan Lal replied.

"*Mohana*, I had gone to my home, and brought my loved and precious things from there." Rajrani exclaimed!

"Did you really go home?"

"Yes; Mohana, I had gone. I reached here just now; and handed over the bag, containing precious things, to your wife." Rajrani exclaimed!

"What precious things did you bring from there?"

"'*Shiv-Puran*', '*Neelmat-Puran*', '*Garud Puran*', 'Vedas', 'Upanishads' and many more things." Rajrani replied in a state of somnolence.

"You handed over the bag to my wife, and not to me, why?"? He asked, just for talking sake.

"*Mohana*, let the Sunrise, I will tell you everything; why hoo-ha at odd hour?" Rajrani muttered. "*Mohana*, it was snowing there; your father was busy reading a book; and he explained to me the 'Vedic' and 'Shaiva-Shakti traditions of Kashmir', benevolent deeds for the mankind, the '*Lok-hit Kriya*', and the benevolent deeds for fellow men, the '*Par-hit Kriya*'", Rajrani added incoherently. Simultaneously, she opened her eyes and realized that her husband had died a year ago. She became overwhelmingly emotional, and started sobbing.

Rajrani's family members woke up, and, in the dead of night, the atmosphere in the community hall again turned pensive. She shut her slow-moving eyelids and started snoring again in her honeyed sleep. Mohan Lal kept staring at her face; he noticed that her face had turned pale, lost its sheen, and that triggered sudden feelings of fear in Mohan Lal's mind.

Rajrani's physical and mental condition made Mohan Lal aware of the grim and inevitable finality; he became excessively conscious that the wind had started to drift; and he realized that the grand family tree would get uprooted at any moment. Fearing that the great desire of her mother, who was ceaselessly craving to return home, shall remain unfulfilled, Mohan Lal became emotionally upset; and tears started streaming down his face.

Mohan Lal's mind was fully occupied by the soul-consuming pain of the loss of his home and living the life of a refugee in his own country, and physical and mental suffering of his mother had pushed him into distress. Quivering with anxiety, he left the community hall to comfort his mind and relax outside for a while to feel the natural breeze and see the twinkling stars.

Mohan Lal started taking deep breaths to control his stress levels and anxiety, but the apprehension of his mother's imminent cessation of existence and the nostalgic sentiments about his beloved homeland were the running undercurrent in his thought process. The heavy load of thoughts, accumulated in his mind, and the dream sequence of his mother had perturbed him immensely. He had realized– that her mother's dreams were nothing but the manifestations of her deepest desires, ambitions and anxieties.

Mohan Lal returned after about an hour, only to see that his mother had traversed to a new form and bliss. Shortly after his interaction with her, Rajrani was no longer alive. Her deep booming laughter and the last words, under the influence of sedating medication, "*Mohana*, let the sunrise, I will tell you everything; why hoo-ha at an odd hour?" continually echoed in Mohan Lal's mind.

After seeing his mother motionless and speechless, Mohan Lal abruptly went into hysterics; and he hit his face with his own hands and banged his head against the wall. Blood oozed out of his contused skull; and he fell unconscious. This alerted and evoked serious emotional reaction among the immediate family members and relatives of Rajrani, and they started breast-beating and crying; and hundreds of inmates of the shelter camp thronged the community hall in the dead of night. In an uncontrolled outburst of emotion, Mohan Lal continually wailed: "O my mother, why did you break your promise of telling me everything; and why didn't you wait for the sun to rise?"

The morning twilight was in sight through the window panes; and the preparations for the cremation of Rajrani had begun. Mohan Lal sobbed continuously; he cried and suffered repeated nervous break downs; and the expressions of the feelings of sadness and strong emotions of his mother moved everybody in the community hall to tears!

Emotionally charged Mohan Lal, in overwhelming sadness and anger, said to his community members who had assembled at the cremation ground, "What you see is not my story alone, every hounded out native of Kashmir, has been experiencing similar and even more horrendous situation, away from their homes and hearths. We need to vigorously fight against the brute forces that have battered our community; we have to reclaim our roots, our homes and the hearths, which is our unalienable right; and if we become lazy, and fail to act appropriately, we all are going to finish in the manner my father, my mother and my brother did."

Tired and exhausted Mohan Lal stayed calm after consigning the mortal remains of his mother to flames, but was lost in thoughts, and swapped old experiences and stories of his mother with friends and relatives. Mohan Lal's mother, Rajrani, throughout her life, fondly addressed Mohan Lal as '*Mohana*', the epithet of the Hindu Gods Shiva and Krishna, and not Mohan Lal; and the word *Mohana* continually reverberated in his mind.

With tears trickling down his cheeks, dejected Mohan Lal said in a choked voice, "My mother loved me more than her life. I have many fond-memories of my mother, but one thing shall haunt me till I die. I lied to her, not once, but umpteen times; and when I think of having lied to her, I get a feeling of venomous swarms and wasps stinging my body. Although our ancestral home, which she would boastfully name as 'my father, Raj Nath's Golden-Lanka', was arsoned within few months of our forced exodus from the homeland, yet I had been telling her that the house was 'in-tact', only to allow her to live happily with brighter hopes."

"Refugees are mothers, fathers, sisters, brothers, children, with the same hopes as us– except that a

twist of fate has bound their lives to a global refugee crisis on an unprecedented scale."

– Khalid Hosseini

10

Displacement Caused Mistrust in Steady Relationships

The incident relates to 'Baisakhi-Day' of the year 2000. At around 9 a.m, Surrender's telephone buzzed; he picked up the phone, only to hear baffled Suman groaning and sobbing: "Please, please, please come to our place immediately; Bansi has locked the exit door of the living room; fixed a nylon-rope in the hook of the ceiling fan; and is bent on either finishing me by strangling or end his own life by hanging."

It took Surinder not more than five minutes to reach the residence of his friend, Bansi. His knocking at the door synchronized with a scary sound of some heavy object hurled at the wall inside; and followed by murmur– Ssssshhhh, the footsteps lumbered clumsily inside the living room before the door was opened for his entry. Bansi's brown eyes were damp with dismay, and his hoarse-sounding wish suggested that he was frenzied.

Surinder sat on a sofa next to Bansi who was continuously rubbing his forehead with the finger tips of his hand and venting out nasal sounds–'hmm---hmm' frequently. Bansi's wife,

Suman, entered the living room from the adjoining room, carrying two tumblers, filled with lemonade, in a small tray; placed one of the two tumblers on the centre table; and offered the other to Surinder. Quivering and trembling with rancour, she gave an angry look to Bansi and Bansi glared at her too. The body language of animosity and antipathy of the husband-wife duo towards each other was sufficient for Bansi to grasp that they had engaged in an altercation before his arrival, and the scattered pieces of broken crockery and mirror in the wardrobe evidenced the severity of violent scuffle that had ensued there. Surinder posed a question to himself: "Why would they do this?" While hundreds of questions were tugging Bansi's brain, he appeared completely shaken, and sweat drops dripped down his forehead, which he wiped out with the back of his hand.

"No, no, no, I can't tolerate stupidity and nonsense anymore; every time you weave crafty stories; and you have made my life distressing and disgraceful", Bansi said to his wife hard-heartedly. Enraged by the words of Bansi, Suman hurriedly retreated into the adjoining room after lifting the broken pieces of mobile-phone, and closed the door forcefully, which made a deafening thud.

Surinder noticed tears pouring down Bansi's face in spurts of enragement and disappointment; and, glistened with emotions, he could not prevent his eyes getting wet. He shut his eyes for a moment, and Bansi touched his feet. "Whatever I have confided to you already, is truth and nothing but the truth; for heaven's sake, please pull me out of the hell." Bansi sighed in despair. Simultaneously, Bansi started screaming in loud shrieks and that made Surinder shiver. For a minute, he gazed into his brown eyes and sat mum, not knowing what to say or do; and after a sigh, he asked, "What happened today, Bansi?"

"Nothing new, my friend; I am crestfallen, tired and dejected; I have been living with pain and humiliation for the last one decade; and it's better for me to live alone because I must accept the truth and not fight it", Bansi screamed and grabbed his arm.

Bansi's words were threatening and chaotic. Surinder wanted to repress his despair; he put his hand on Bansi's head, and moved the hand back and forth to comfort him. Bansi, in a choked voice, said, "My friend, I am an ordinary human being, but at the very first sight of many young friends of this most wicked and crafty woman, I invariably get a strange feeling that they have striped me naked, and are spitting at my body. Her day-to-day manipulations have made me like a chained bulldog." Instantly, his face screwed up in severe anguish and he exclaimed, "I am a mad man and can't compromise!" He took a deep sigh and added, "She is enslaved by the desire of sensual pleasures; her external physical senses are not under-control; and she becomes violent to deter me from becoming a hurdle in her schemes of fulfilling aphrodisiac urges."

Face to face with his wife, Bansi gave a complete account of a number of instances which had happened or brewed before his eyes, over the years, without overstressing, to afford Surinder an insight regarding the conduct of Suman. In addition to serious admonishments, on many occasions, he had given her veiled warnings to shun the perilous path of immoral physical-gratification. In support of the grave charges of 'immoral conduct', Bansi had given to her rational reasoning and proof, on umpteen times, but every time deviant Suman turned violent to detour the issue.

While Bansi was narrating his tale of woes and pathos to Surinder, Suman intervened and reacted twice. At one point, she said to her husband, "please mind your language, and have regard for human dignity. I am a human being and not a 'commodity'; I love animals, birds and trees; I love a whole lot of people who I am acquainted with including my family members and our common relatives; do you mean to say that I am attracted towards all for physical gratification?" At another point, she said, "In a husband-wife relationship, respect for 'human dignity' is paramount, next comes the ideal social and moral behavior; and suspecting the faithfulness of marriage partner on mere assumptions, presumptions and fallible perceptions is like burying the husband-wife sacrosanct relationship in a grave."

Bansi was a commerce graduate and had a flourishing 'Tour and Travel' business in Kashmir valley. He was a close friend of Surinder from childhood days. As Surinder knew him, he was a 'perfect Man' and in deep need of being needed. He possessed a great sense of humor and intense curiosity; his enthusiasm had no bounds; and the only drawback in him was that he was blunt, and never expressed himself in a tolerant and socially accepted manner.

Suman was a Postgraduate; as a student of History, she had a thorough grasp of Kashmir's past; and was working as a teacher in a private educational institute. She was born in an affluent Dhar family and was highly impressed by Rupabhawani, the daughter of a deeply religious Kashmiri Pandit, Madhav Dhar.

Suman had memorized most of the mystic and spiritual *Vaaks* of Lal-Ded and the *Shruks* of Nund Reshi. She was warm, bright, action-oriented, and driven by the desire to be loved and admired. Bansi and Suman had entered into wedlock in the year 1985. The couple owned a mansion with a vast garden in the posh civil lines area of Srinagar city in Kashmir valley. They were indigenous minority Hindus of Kashmir, 'the *Battas*'; and Suman prided herself as 'Daughter of *Vitasta*'. River Jhelum is the changed name of 'Vitasta'.

Bansi and his family were part of the minuscule minority community of the valley, hounded out of their homeland in 1990, living as 'refugees in their own country' in one of the Shelter camps established by the administrative apparatus of the state.

Herding a family of five, including Bansi's mother, in tented accommodation on the outskirts of Jammu city, was a horrible experience for Bansi and Suman as they could not afford to achieve even a small measure of their earlier life styles. They started living in a miserable condition, only to struggle for their survival in a new environment. Thrown as they were into an alien atmosphere, Bansi's family was completely marooned in the ocean of tension and anxiety for the loss of 'home and hearth'. Financial and business worries, unsuitable living environment, disappointment and loss of privacy had given birth to their mental disturbance, and attitudinal and behavioral changes.

After living in tented accommodation for more than a year, Bansi with his family had been shifted to one-room tenement; and towards the end of 2008, he sold his Srinagar house and shifted to a 2-bedroom rented accommodation on the outskirts of Jammu city.

Surinder had close family ties with Bansi's family; he had been observing the quivering movements in the relationship of husband-wife duo for quite some time, but was not aware that the situation had reached a flash point; and after noticing a nylon rope hanging in the hook of ceiling-fan, he could perceive an imminent volcanic activity. The manifestations were quite visible and he was curious enough to know the genesis of the problem.

Surinder had a full-day hectic interaction with both; and his attitude was not of agreeing with Bansi or admiring Suman. As a family friend, Surinder wanted the couple not to take any extreme step in the heat of rage or provocation, but that appeared imminent. He wanted to do everything possible to save the relationship from break-up. "What could be done in the given situation, Surinder posed a question to himself? Instantly the reply came from his inner-self: "Don't leave them alone in any case, they need vigorous counseling."

A wonderful idea struck Bansi's mind instantly–he asked both of them to get up, lock their house and accompany him, and they complied unhesitatingly. After about one-hour drive, Surinder, Bansi and his wife, Suman, reached an *Ashram*. It was 4 p.m. Swami Ji, the Seer, sporting a long tuft of hair and flying-beard, attired in white cotton-gown and white woolen-cap, was Seated in *Padm-Aasana*, crossed-legs and straightened upper-limbs posture, in the main hall. About a dozen enlightenment-seekers were sitting at his feet, silently sharing his presence. Surinder along with the couple also sat there after wishing the *Swami Ji* with folded hands.

What Surinder knew about the *Swami Ji* was a celibate, who fully renounced the worldly pleasures, left his home 45 years ago at the age of 15 for spiritual practices under the guidance of his Guru, the Mater. And, what he had observed in the *Ashram*, during his earlier *Darshanas,* the meetings, with *Swami Ji* was whosoever sat before him, he was utterly with him, focused and attentive; and his advice could be bitter and painful, but he never condemned anybody; and would always speak with compassion.

After closing his eyes for nearly 5 minutes, *Swami Ji* peeped into the eyes of Bansi, and posed a question: "What are you analyzing and fantasizing?" Bansi hesitatingly said with a fake smile, "Oh, umm; you know everything, *Swami Ji.* I am a miserable person."

Swami Ji said to Bansi instantly with a smile, "Hmmmmm, a miserable person is a sinner because only the sins make a person miserable–the sins may be of your past or present." He instantly posed yet another question to Bansi: "Why do you want to escape from the reality?"

Bansi fumbled, "Hm, hm." Quoting a vaakh of Lallishvari *Yogini*, *Swami ji* said to Bansi with laughter, "If the mind strays into illusions like a donkey in fields, it will eat up the saffron–the precious knowledge; hear me with complete attention; and ponder over it with a cool mind–extra-seriousness is a serious disease and your cynicism, misery and despair are the outcome of your over-possessive attitude, you need to drop the misery. In true love, the mad passion for possessing the person is quite natural and understandable, but stupid ways and means to sort out problems and issues with one's partner make the other person feel guilty, alienated and irrelevant, which aggravates the problem further". He recited a verse of chapter 13 of Bhagavad-Gita and said, "The Lord means to say that on account of man's close association with his wife, son, home, body and wealth etc, he is unusually attached with these. Even after developing dispassion, the hidden feeling of attachment persists." In an indirect reference to Bansi, Swami JI posed a question to one of the persons in attendance, "Isn't it quite imperative that you give energy, protection, care and security to the loved one so that the person does not go farther away in a state of helplessness?"

After the tea break of about half an hour, the discourse restarted and *Swami Ji* posed a volley of questions to Bansi's wife:

"What is your name?" *Swami Ji* asked.

"Suman, Swami Ji."

"Oh; I see; you are a 'flower'; beautiful; benevolent–all original– tremendous energy– loving energy! Look; I can understand that you are a fine, sober, intelligent and humble creature; your intelligence and sensitiveness are the root cause of psychological disturbance that you suffer from; do you take psychotherapeutic medicines?" *Swami Ji* said.

"Yes, Swami Ji." Suman replied.

"Mind you, psychotherapy will do no trick, only the meditation will help to overcome problems." Swami Ji said.

"Please guide me, *Swami Ji.*" Suman replied.

"Meditation–only through that, you will find the real meaning of life!" Swami Ji said.

"Please allow me to remain under your feet, Swami Ji. I feel relieved!" Suman said.

After closing his eyes for about a minute, Swami Ji said, "OK; you can stay here with your husband for a few days, but both of you shall have to live as celibates and participate in morning and evening prayers regularly."

"I will do that, *Swami Ji*!" Suman replied.

Swami Ji wanted to know Bansi's reaction, and he panned his looks at him. Instant came his reaction with hands folded. "I will do whatever you ask me to do; I need your blessings, *Swami Ji.*" Bansi said in submission.

"OK, Krishna will take care of you both! He will take care of every displaced person of Kashmir– only the fleeting and illusory 'Time' will decide appropriately at the appropriate time!" *Swami Ji* said.

The couple stayed in the *Ashram* for one complete month; the meditation helped them to develop deep inner contact with each other; they restarted the journey of life together; and loved the very joy of the journey, and the opening of the flower of harmony in their relationship!

And, the Seer's counseling and intervention brought complete harmony in the relationship of husband-wife!

> *"Refugees didn't just escape a place. They had to escape a thousand memories until they'd put enough time and distance between them and their misery to wake to a better day."*
>
> **– Nadia Hashimi**

www.ingramcontent.com/pod-product-compliance
Lightning Source LLC
Chambersburg PA
CBHW022157160726
48282CB00024B/230
* 9 7 8 9 3 9 3 0 2 9 3 1 7 *